THE COMPETITIVE DYNAMICS OF CONTAINER SHIPPING

To my wife

The Competitive Dynamics of Container Shipping

SIDNEY GILMAN
Marine Transport Centre,
University of Liverpool

Gower

British Library Cataloguing in Publication Data

Gilman, Sidney
  The competitive dynamics of container shipping.
  1. Containerization
  I. Title
  387.5'442   HE596

  ISBN 0-566-00573-5

Published by
Gower Publishing Company Limited,
Gower House, Croft Road, Aldershot, Hants GU11 3HR,
England

Reprinted 1986

Printed and bound in Great Britain by
Antony Rowe Limited, Chippenham, Wiltshire

Contents

Figures   vii

Tables   ix

Acknowledgements   xi

Glossary   xiii

1   Early History of the Conference System   1

2   The Container Revolution   7

3   Ship Type and Market Role   15

4   Economies of Scale   33

5   The Logistics of Container Transport Networks   43

6   Classical Models of Conference Behaviour   49

7   Market Function in the Intermodal Age   55

8   Market Profiles   61

9   Regulation in the United States - 1961 - 1982   83

10   The Movement for Regulatory Reform   95

11   The UN Liner Code, CENSA Code and EEC Competition Rules   109

12   Summary and Conclusions   121

Bibliography   133

Figures

		Page
2.1	The Re-structuring of Conventional Markets	12
3.1	Profile and Section Drawings of the Cellular Containership Fort Royal	16
3.2	Profile and Hold Section of the Semi Containership Menelaus	17
3.3	Profile of the Semi Containership Corinna Drescher	18
3.4	Profile of the Deep Sea Ro-ro Ship Nedlloyd Rouen	20
3.5	Profile of the Anro Class Container Ro-ro Ships	22
3.6	Profile of the Boxer Class Container Ro-ro Ships	23
3.7	General Arrangement of the Bulk Container Carrier Helen	25
3.8	Profile of the Skaugran - A Large Ro-ro Ship for Semi Bulks	27
4.1	Economies of Size at Various Speeds for a Family of Cellular Containerships	35
4.2	Economies of Size at Various Speeds (Taking Account of Containers and Inventories)	35
12.1	The Evolution of Regulatory Regimes	128

Tables

		Page
2.1	Movement of Unit Load Cargo from Britain to Europe	10
2.2	Estimated Growth of Deep Sea Container Capacity 1978-84	13
3.1	The World Wide Distribution of Deep Sea Container Capacity in 1980	30
3.2	Container Capacity of Ro-ro Ships by Route: 1980	31
3.3	Container Capacity of Semi and Bulk Container Ships	32
4.1	Costs per OOO TEU Miles for a Family of Cellular Containerships	36
4.2	Ship Costs/TEU in Port at a Range of Handling Rates	38
4.3	Ship Costs at Sea and in Port	40
5.1	Mother or Feeder Ship Costs	47
7.1	Rates of Escalation of Ship Capital and Operating Costs	57
8.1	Europe to Australasia	63
8.2	NW Europe - South Africa	65
8.3	NW Europe to the Far East	68
8.4	Mediterranean to the Far East	69
8.6	NW Europe US Gulf and West Coast	74
8.7	The Trans Pacific Routes	76
8.8	US East and West Coast to the Far East	78

Acknowledgements

This book arises from a desire to apply the results of earlier work on liner shipping (which concentrated on the questions of ship choice and transport geography) to the problems of market function. In particular I wished to contribute to the long standing debate on the role of liner conferences, taking account of the particular features of containers and intermodal transport systems. As it happens the present time is one of particular importance with respect to developments in the systems which regulate the functioning of conferences. The UN Liner Code is at last about to enter into force, there is great activity in the United States in the attempt to reform the regulatory regime and the EEC Commission is also beginning to consider the nature of possible competition rules for the Community as a whole. The book thus proceeds from basic analysis of the operating characteristics of container systems, through a consideration of market and conference function, to a study of a number of container routes, and finally to developments and issues in regulatory policy.

In carrying out the analysis of container routes I am grateful to the Science & Engineering Research Council for funding a research project at the Marine Transport Centre on the deployment of deep sea container carrying ships. I am also indebted to Mr. John Fossey for his cheerful persistence and hard work in producing the basic statistical material required from Voyage Records. In interpreting this I have made extensive use of market reports published in the industry press. Turning to the area of regulatory policy I have been greatly assisted by the UWIST Report for CENSA and also by Mr. J. Davies, one of the co-authors of that report, who provided me with extensive background source material on some of the legal aspects of the US regulatory regime. I would also like to thank Mr. Robert Ellsworth and his colleagues at the Federal Maritime Commission, Mr. Stanley Sher of Billig, Sher & Jones, and staff of the CENSA Secretariat in London. The views expressed here are, however, my own, as is the responsibility for any errors.

Finally, I would like to thank Mrs. Marjorie Brash for carrying out the painstaking work of producing the text and her equanimity in the face of the changes made in it during the course of preparation.

Glossary

Block stow: Unitised cargo stowed in blocks chiefly semi bulk cargoes but includes containers when not in cell guides.

Break bulk: Non unitised general cargo.

Cellular containership: Ship equipped with cell guides in all holds to facilitate container handling by lo-lo methods.

CENSA: Council of European and Japanese National Shipowners' Associations.

COAR: Co-operatively organised and appropriately rationalised.

Container ro-ro ship: Containership with ro-ro access to one or more decks, with dedicated space for the stowage of containers worked by lo-lo methods.

Conventional system: The pre container method of handling general cargo.

CSG: Consultative Shipping Group. Belgium Finland, Denmark, Federal Republic of Germany, France, Greece, Italy, Japan, the Netherlands, Norway, Spain, Sweden, UK.

dwt: Dead weight tonnes.

General cargo: The varied cargoes moving in the liner trades. They are in a wide range of parcel sizes, but always less than full ship lots.

Hatch covers: That (re)movable part of the weather deck which covers each hold, protecting it from the elements. Cellular ships have removable lids known as 'pontoon' hatch covers. Semi containerships may have folding hatch covers.

xiii

Landbridge:	A through transport movement involving two waterborne shipments at either end of a central road/rail hauled movement.
Liner service:	A frequent regular service on an established itinerary.
Lo-lo:	Lift-on/lift-off.
Mini-bridge:	A through movement under a single bill of lading which transfers at the unloading port to a train service serving a rail terminal in some other port city.
Multi-port operation:	A route itinerary having numerous port calls at either end of the route.
Panamax ship:	A ship, the dimensions of which are constrained in size by the Gatun Locks of the Panama Canal. Sometimes referred to as third generation.
Reefer container:	Refrigerated container.
Ro-ro:	Roll-on/roll-off.
Ro-ro/containership:	Ship used for carrying containers, the handling of which is accomplished by ro-ro methods.
Self-sustaining:	Refers to ships with onboard gear (craneage) or ramps and fork lift trucks or trailers, giving the capability to load/discharge independently of shore based facilities.
Self-trimming:	A bulk cargo hold so designed that cargo will flow to an even depth.
Semi-bulk cargo:	Unitised or self unitising cargo in large volume, e.g. timber, forest products, steel, sometimes expanded to embrace cars and liquids like chemicals and oils.
Semi-containership:	Evolved version of the conventional liner. Non cellular but with reasonably good container capacity.
Ships' gear:	Craneage carried onboard ship.

Tank top:	Lowest deck of a ship (immediately above the ballast and fuel tanks).
TEU:	Twenty foot equivalent unit.
Tramp:	A ship employed on a voyage by voyage basis to haul bulk and/or semi bulk cargoes.

1 Early history of the conference system

CONFERENCE ORIGINS

Collective agreements on shipping freight rates and services have a
history which has been traced back to as early as 1450, but it is
generally agreed that the conference system as we know it today grew up
in the last quarter of the 19th century. The main formative element
was clearly the development of the steamship and of the new engines
which increased speed and reliability and reduced bunker requirements.
This affected scale in two ways. First, it had the reliability to
make liner services possible, so that the unit of production became the
fleet rather than the ship, and second it allowed a substantial increase
in ship size. In the late 19th century the scale required to run liner
services could only be provided by co-operation and this took the form
of the loose collective monopolies known as conferences. There was of
course rather more to it. In particular the period was one of substantial overcapacity brought about partly by the size of the new steamships, partly by residual competition from sailing ships and partly by
the opening of the Suez Canal. It has been shown that whilst UK trade
was increasing at a rate of only some $2\frac{1}{2}$ per cent per annum the capacity
of ships registered in the UK was increasing at over 5 per cent.
(Deakin and Seward 1973). Thus shipowners needed to combine to protect
themselves from excessive competition as well as to obtain sufficient
scale to run a liner service. At the time these two elements hung
together, in that the need for scale which led to the formation of
conferences also served as a barrier to competition from outsiders.
The first conference was formed on the UK Calcutta trade in 1875 and
this was followed by rapid developments on other routes so that the
conference system became the predominant form of market organisation in
liner shipping.

THE DEVELOPMENT OF THE CLOSED RATIONALISING CONFERENCE

The essence of the early developments in UK trades was that shipping
lines agreed a common set of rates between two ranges of ports and
supported this by tying arrangements with shippers. These took the
form of contractual arrangements which embodied either dual rate
contracts, where exclusive users of the conference paid a lower rate
than occasional users, or the rather stronger deferred rebates, where
the difference between contract and non contract rates was returned
after an interval of some six months. At the same time there were
methods of regulating capacity and the conference would combat competition from outsiders with rate wars, either by all conference ships,

or preferably by selective attack with fighting ships, if this were allowed. The growth and development of three UK conferences has been traced up to the 1960s, showing the detailed differences between them and the difficulties they often faced, particularly in the depressed inter-war years. (Deakin and Seward 1973). Thus in the Far Eastern Freight Conference in the 1920s and 1930s there was severe competition from outsiders many of whom had to be admitted to the conference. Finding it difficult to obtain adequate market shares they requested freedom to fix their own rates, a request which was turned down by the conference as breaching an important principle. However, from the early 1920s there were severe problems in respect of underquoting of the conference tariff. After much discussion a solution was attempted by the formation of an earnings pool but even this did not succeed and in the 1930s the conference adopted an internal policing and penalties scheme.

The Australian trade also faced a number of problems in the inter war period including a rapid growth of terminal costs and poor cargo balance, leading to excessive multi-port calling northbound. An excess of capacity also developed on the route leading to a decline in freight rates so that by the late 1920s most lines were making losses. In that year there was an increase in outbound rates and Australian exporters, fearful that this was a prelude to an increase in rates in the homeward trade, asked the government to intervene. This was the beginning of the long term involvement of the Australian government in shipping and of the development of a special form of rationalising closed conference. This developed in stages over a quite long period of time. The first stage, which followed the request for intervention, was the formation of Producer Boards and a Council of Exporters. These bodies were empowered to negotiate agreements for Australian exports, wool operating under a deferred rebate system and all other commodities under contracts. Shippers also provided the outbound conference with forecasts of their expected throughputs, although in many cases these proved to be wildly inaccurate.

In 1955, following a further government intervention in rate negotiation, a system was established whereby rates would be set according to a formula based on shipping costs, the level of costs being verified by the supply of voyage accounts to independent accountants. Following this in the mid 1960s under the auspices of the Australian Trade Practices Act, shippers formed themselves into a single body, the Australia Europe Shippers Association (AESA) the lines having to agree to negotiate with that body on rates and to provide all reasonable information as the basis. At the same time the Australian government brought considerable pressure to bear upon the conference lines to rationalise itineraries as an alternative to rate increases. This required a revenue pool and operational co-operation between lines and provided a basis upon which the lines were able to build when they formed the consortias which containerised the route from Europe to Australia.

The switch to containers was the high point in the operation of closed rationalising conferences. First of all there was an increase in ship size which required further integration, accomplished in many cases by the formation of consortia. Second there was an opportunity to start with a clean sheet with a new technology which in itself was a strong rationalising influence, and finally a period of relative freedom from outside competition. The major closed conferences on the routes from north west Europe to Australia, South Africa and the Far East undoubtedly did a very good job during this period, but they were operating in favourable circumstances, and as will be shown later competitive influences reasserted themselves.

Conferences have always been viewed with suspicion and as early as 1909 in the UK the Royal Commission on Shipping Rings investigated conference activities. It found the conference system to be necessary for the provision of liner services and allowed a self regulating system of closed conferences immunity from the laws against monopolistic practice. The review of closed conferences began again in the 1960's involving shippers and shipping lines in Europe and Japan together with the developing countries. Eventually the debate began to centre around Codes of Conduct for Liner Conferences. The lines of the developed countries produced the CENSA code in 1971, but this was not acceptable in developing countries, and after some twenty years of discussion and negotiation in UNCTAD, a UN Liner Code is about to come into force. Although many developing countries have been highly critical of conferences the UNCTAD Code depends for its effective operation on powerful conferences operating cargo sharing arrangements.

THE OPEN CONFERENCES OF THE US TRADES

In the United States there are two distinct eras in conference history, the first from the late 19th century when the conferences were formed up to 1961 and the second from 1961 to the present day.

In the early years of their existence in US trades conferences should have been illegal under the Sherman Act, as they were business combinations or conspiracies engaging in a variety of illegal practices. But the courts had not taken this view and in 1907 a conference which had used both deferred rebates and fighting ships was held not to be unreasonably restraining trade. However, the consensus of Congressional opinion was that conferences were illegal and following some attempts to legislate for enforcement of the anti-trust laws, the House of Representatives directed its Committee on Merchant Marine and Fisheries under the chairmanship of Alexander to investigate conferences with a view to recommending to Congress legislation which would provide stability in ocean transport. The Alexander Report issued in 1914 became the basis of regulatory policy as embodied in the 1916 Shipping Act.

The Alexander Committee found that conferences provided great benefits in the form of regularity and frequency of sailings, stability of rates and economy of operation, and also that they led to equal treatment of shippers and elimination of secret arrangements and underhand methods of discrimination. It also believed that in the absence of conferences there would be a period of rate wars leading to eventual monopoly. It viewed shipping conferences as the only alternative to this, but since they created a form of monopoly liable to abuse, recommended that they should be subject to government regulation.

The Shipping Act allowed the formation of open conferences. Fighting

3

ships and deferred rebates were specifically prohibited, but although
dual rate contracts were not mentioned it was tacitly assumed they
would be allowed.   The main provision of the Act was that conferences
were to be under the supervision of a regulatory authority, the Federal
Maritime Board, which would monitor conference agreements to ensure that
they complied with certain standards.   These regulatory standards,
which were incorporated in Sections 14 and 15 of the Shipping Act contained certain basic safeguards for shippers and also set out to protect
the interests of the United States in a world in which it was concerned
about the potential level of competition.   Specifically the standards
stated that conference agreements were not to be 'unjustly discriminatory
or unfair between carriers, shippers, exporters, importers or ports; or
between exporters of the US and their foreign competitors; or to operate
to the detriment of the commerce of the United States.   However, every
agreement found to be lawful under the Act was exempted from the anti
trust laws.   The FMB also had responsibility for promoting the US
Merchant Marine and indeed shortly after the end of World War I it was
given the job of operating for profit the large fleet built up during
the war pending its transfer to private ownership.   In this capacity it
became a member of the North Atlantic Conferences and also of the closed
European Far East Freight Conference.   Even after the transfer of the
fleet the Board concentrated on promotional activities, and in 1936 was
given the responsibility for the administration of subsidies to the US
fleet.   Further to this, although the Board generally required conferences to be open, it had the right to allow them to refuse membership
when to grant it would be economically damaging, either because of lack
of financial stability of the trade, overtonnaging in the trade, or where
a line sought to take a profit from a trade which it had not helped to
develop.   These conditions of course are very similar to those which
the closed conferences use in reviewing applications for membership.
During the period up to 1961 the regulatory agency pursued only 127
cases of violation, only half of which led to any form of regulatory
order.   There were only four cases of reparation and six cases referred
to the Department of Justice, none of which led to prosecutions.   (J.
Davies 1978).   Thus although the US system ostensibly favoured open
conferences its operation was not very different from the closed conference system operated by the main European lines.

In 1958 the regulatory system again came under government scrutiny,
partly because of a growing controversy surrounding the use of dual
rate contracts and partly because of the increasing interest of the
Department of Justice in ocean shipping.   Dual rates had not been
specifically mentioned in the 1916 Shipping Act but they had become
common practice.   They were challenged by the Isbrandtsen Company in
a long drawn out case, and in 1958 in The Federal Maritime Board v
Isbrandtsen Company it was held that dual rate contracts were retaliation by discriminatory method and therefore contrary to Section 14 of
the Act.   This led to a great deal of uncertainty as it was not clear
whether the decision applied to all dual rate contracts or merely those
which could be interpreted as predatory devices stifling non conference
competition.   In an attempt to clarify the situation the House of
Representatives asked its Committee of Merchant Marine and Fisheries
under the Chairmanship of Representative Bonner to make a study of
conferences with special reference to the dual rate system.   At the
same time the Department of Justice started its own investigation in

the Celler Committee, which was charged with the study of conferences and FMB regulation in the context of a general review of monopoly practices, whilst the Senate also formed an investigatory body in its Sub-Committee of Merchant Marine and Fisheries.   The investigations lasted three years with the Celler Committee making a strong attack on conferences, whilst the Bonner Committee supported them.   The Senate Committee also gave general support to provide a consensus in favour of continuation of a regime of conferences operating under regulatory supervision, but with supervision being much more rigorous.   This was the approach eventually followed in the comprehensive revision of the Shipping Act embodied in Public Law 87-346.   The regulatory regime was re-organised with responsibility for promotion of the Merchant Marine being taken away from the FMB, leaving a new Federal Maritime Commission free to concentrate on regulation alone, and the regulatory provisions of the Shipping Act were strengthened.   Dual rate contracts were, however, allowed and it was the intention of Congress that the industry should operate behind a broad anti trust shield.   However, during the 1960s and 1970s, as a result of actions in the courts and the continued attentions of the Department of Justice, there was an erosion of this anti trust immunity, and the regulatory regime began to operate in a harsh and arbitrary manner which interfered severely with the operation of the industry and raised serious issues of comity with trading partners.   As a result of this, together with the desire to improve the functioning of domestic liner companies and reduce the burden of sub-sidies, a movement for regulatory reform developed in the 1970s.

OBJECTIVES

With the UN Code expected to come into force in 1983 and impending regulatory reform in the US the liner shipping industry is again on the threshold of a substantial change in its regulatory environment. Because of the enormous changes in the industry in the last fifteen years much of the older literature on the subject is no longer strictly applicable.   Certainly there needs to be some reconsideration in the light of an understanding of the technology and operating pattern of the container shipping industry and the experience of its major markets in recent years.

The objectives of this book are to investigate the functioning of the liner shipping industry, as it has developed under the influence of containerisation, and consider the questions of conference organisation, regulation and shipping policy generally in the light of this analysis. The early chapters start with the characteristics of supply and demand. This leads in to a discussion of market operation and a review of major markets in the early 1980s;   then finally to a consideration of major issues with respect to shipping policy.

2 The container revolution

The link between the introduction of steamships and the formation of liner conferences was discussed in Chapter 1. Following this revolutionary change the period up to the middle of the 20th century was one of slow technological evolution. Such progress as there was, related chiefly to construction techniques and improvements in the design of engines. These led to reductions in steel weight and in fuel consumption, but neither had any significant effect on the functioning of the market. When revolutionary change did eventually come it was from a new direction, that of the technology of cargo handling.

The labour intensive cargo handling methods of the conventional system were incapable of much improvement. Power cranes became available in the 19th century and their use increased steadily, but this had no significant effect on the jobs of stowing and securing cargo, particularly as hatches remained small and movement into the wings of the ship remained a manual operation. As a result cargo handling rates remained static at an average of up to about 400 tonnes per day for mixed general cargo, and up to 1,200 tonnes per day for homogeneous cargoes like bagged grain moved in large volume. In fact it was the tramp ships which achieved high rates, whilst the liners with their more complicated itineraries and mix of cargoes, operated at the lower end of the range. Largely because of slow handling rates ship size remained within the limit of 14,000 dwt., and there was a general similarity between tramps and liners in terms of size, cargo spaces and cargo handling methods. As wage rates increased in the developed countries cargo handling costs came to represent an ever increasing proportion of round trip costs and the long periods of time that ships spent in port also became a focus of concern. In the US for example, by 1960 stevedoring costs alone accounted for about 60 per cent of the total cost of movement from port gate to port gate, and when ship time was taken into account the port sector accounted for 80 per cent of the total. Solutions to this problem were sought from the early 1950s onwards. There were a number of modifications in liners allowing palletisation and the use of fork lift trucks in the holds, but this was only moderately successful. Meanwhile the first experiments were being made with cargo handling units between ten and twenty times larger than those of the conventional system.

The most dramatic changes occurred when a large increase in size of unit, a radical simplification of port operations and integration with inland modes were simultaneously achieved by the conceptually simple expedient of taking the whole of a road trailer aboard ship. It could be towed aboard, or the wheels could be taken off and it could be lifted aboard;

the first approach leading to roll-on roll-off systems and the second to the cellular container system. The process began in 1951, when TMT took a converted truck body as deck cargo from Miami to Puerto Rico. It was taken up in the US by Sea-Land and Matson, who led the development of the cellular container system and by Australian, Scandinavian and British companies, who participated in this and also explored the possibilities of roll-on roll-off ships and methods of handling containers. Whilst this was progressing new specialised ships were also being designed for the large flows of those cargoes which did not need containers in order to be handled efficiently in large units. These included 'open hatch' bulk carriers for steel, timber and forest products; car carriers; parcel tankers for oils and fats, and some barge carriers which linked into the inland waterway systems of the USA. In some of these ships and some bulk carriers a supplementary container carrying capability was introduced which allowed operation in the liner market. Finally, the traditional liner developed a container capability evolving eventually into the semi-containership. The three groups of ships operating as container carriers are listed below: the first two have replaced the old liners, whilst the third may operate as liners but they often concentrate on bulks and offer only fringe competition in liner markets.

BROAD CLASSIFICATION OF CONTAINER CARRYING SHIPS

Pure container systems

    The cellular container system
    Full container ships using ro-ro systems, either alone
    or in combination with lo-lo handling or the cellular system

Flexible systems for containers plus non containerised cargoes

    Semi-container
    Full ro-ro
    Container ro-ro

Specialised systems with supplementary container capability

    Bulk container
    Open hatch bulk carriers
    Large ro-ros for semi-bulks
    Barge aboard ship

Conventional

    Tramps and liners with limited container capability

Some of the important technical features of these ships are discussed in Chapter 3, but here the focus remains on the structure of the market.

THE COMPOSITION OF DEMAND IN THE LINER SECTOR

The varied composition of the liner market is illustrated in Table 2.1

which shows flows of unitised cargo between the UK and Continental Europe and also the penetration obtained of the different categories of cargo.   There are great differences between trading hinterlands which affect the composition of flows but certain general characteristics of the liner market can be discussed.   First, in spite of the existence of the specialised bulk and semi-bulk ships referred to above, bulk cargoes retain a great importance within the liner sector.   These may include cereals, fertilisers and animal feeding stuffs, as well as the more familiar products like steel, timber and cars.   In these sectors cargo tends to be handled by a limited number of large shippers. Following this there are some large items within the general cargo sector proper, and many of these are also handled by a small number of shippers, or (in the case of agricultural products), export marketing boards.   Finally, there is a long tail to the market consisting of hundreds, if not thousands, of shippers with small and medium sized consignments.   A rule of thumb often used is that 20 per cent of shippers are responsible for 80 per cent of the market.

One of the accepted maxims about the liner sector is that demand is distributed among a large number of shippers, none of whom has suffic- ient cargo to fill a ship.   This is still technically correct but too much weight should not be given to it, because there are quite large concentrations of market power in the hands of big shippers and marketing boards.   Their attitudes towards conferences are important and in some cases they have followed deliberate policies of supporting outsiders to increase the competitiveness of the market.

SOME BENCHMARKS ON TOTAL DEMAND

The introduction of containers was followed by a period of very rapid growth, but it is necessary to distinguish between the growth of a particular system and that of the market as a whole.   There was very rapid growth in container traffics, but the re-structuring of the market could well have led to a reduction in the size of the liner sector as semi-bulk cargoes moved into specialised ships.

The characteristic pattern when a new system is introduced is for a slow initial learning period, followed by a period of explosive growth, after which the rate falls back to the natural level.   This is shown in the 'S' curve drawn in Figure 2.1 which also illustrates the way in which conventional markets have been re-organised. For the world as a whole a series of such curves are superimposed to create the total pattern of demand, although in some cases, as with developing countries the prep- aratory phase may be very extended.   However, conventional systems can only carry a limited number of containers and as penetration rises a break point is reached at which new tonnage is required.   At this point there is a strong incentive to switch completely both for operational simplicity and also to provide a sufficient throughput to sustain the investment in the new system.   For this reason even in developing countries container markets can have a burst of explosive growth.

The estimated total of container capacity on deep and medium sea routes in 1980 is 14,300,000 TEUs. (Pearson and Fossey, 1983).   A high proportion of this is on a handful of major routes between the developed nations (including here the newly industrialising nations of the Far East

Table 2.1
Movement of Unit Load Cargo from Britain to Europe (1978)

EXPORTS

Commodity	Total Movement (Tonnes)	Unit Load Penetration %	Unitised Movement (Tonnes)
Meat & meat preparations	194,627	94	182,949
Dairy products	247,750	81	200,677
Cereals	2,707,219	9	243,649
Fruit & vegetables	429,060	43	184,495
Animal feeding stuffs	270,661	40	108,264
Miscellaneous foodstuffs	435,439	72	313,516
Beverages	278,571	74	206,142
Live animals	96,473	76	92,614
Forest products	353,489	68	240,372
Ores & scrap	1,707,608	8	136,608
Fertilisers & minerals	9,946,378	4	397,855
Oils & Fats	125,317	56	70,177
Miscellaneous basic materials	232,113	87	201,938
Organic chemicals	30,766,976	2	615,339
Inorganic chemicals incl. manufactured fertiliser	1,387,422	30	416,226
Plastics	596,348	88	524,786
Other chemicals	866,079	73	632,237
Textiles	299,179	83	248,318
Non-met. mineral manufactures	868,883	70	608,218
Iron & steel	2,275,020	32	728,006
Non-ferrous metals	462,114	54	230,101
Metal manufactures	426,648	76	324,252
Power generating machinery	162,806	77	125,360
Specialised machinery	448,971	63	282,851
Metal working machinery	75,676	50	37,838
General machinery	295,349	74	218,558
Electrical machinery	247,646	82	203,071
Transport equipment	972,320	58	563,945
Wood & cork manufacture	87,429	89	77,811
Paper & board manufacture	354,236	86	304,642
Other manufactured goods	617,493	20	123,498

Table 2.1 (contd.)

IMPORTS

Commodity	Total Movement (Tonnes)	Unit Load Penetration %	Unitised Movement (Tonnes)
Meat & meat preparations	780,374	99	772,570
Dairy products	321,277	97	311,638
Cereals	2,811,541	20	562,308
Fruit & vegetables	2,387,158	67	1,599,395
Animal feeding stuffs	951,843	14	133,258
Miscellaneous foodstuffs	850,219	70	595,153
Beverages	707,318	64	452,683
Live animals	166,112	47	78,072
Forest products	4,832,231	8	386,578
Ores & scrap	460,631	3	13,818
Fertilisers & minerals	3,769,970	8	301,597
Oils & fats	369,011	29	107,013
Miscellaneous basic materials	368,956	77	284,096
Organic chemicals	28,997,779	$1\frac{1}{2}$	434,966
Inorganic chemicals inc. manufactured fertiliser	2,013,132	20	402,626
Plastics	868,500	90	781,650
Other chemicals	764,103	53	404,974
Textiles	404,642	95	384,409
Non-met. mineral manufactures	771,017	84	647,654
Iron & steel	3,686,227	13	479,209
Non-ferrous metals	648,467	46	298,295
Metal manufactures	278,725	88	245,278
Power generating machinery	102,139	87	88,860
Specialised machinery	294,923	72	212,344
Metal working machinery	60,469	83	50,189
General machinery	253,718	93	235,957
Transport equipment	1,060,306	35	371,107
Wood & cork manufacture	1,252,101	43	538,403
Paper & board manufacture	3,012,617	28	843,532
Other manufactured goods	711,583	93	661,772

Source: UK Customs and Excise

and the major oil producers.) Most of these markets must be now almost
fully containerised and future growth will clearly be at the natural
rate of increased cargo generation. On a few routes this can be as
high as 10 per cent for some years, and rates of this order have
recently been sustained among the major oil producers and also on routes
from the Far East to Europe and the USA. But in some cases high rates
of growth are a reflection of the competitiveness of particular countries and there tend to be compensating reductions on other routes. The
average for liner cargo as a whole probably does not exceed five per
cent per annum and it could well be much less than this in the present
period of recession.

Figure 2.1

The Re-structuring of Conventional Markets

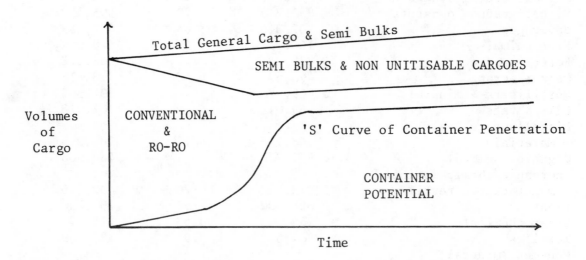

There is still some growth to come from increasing container penetration
in developing countries, but this will be of a much smaller order of
magnitude than that which has already taken place on major routes.   The
International Financial Statistics of the IMF show that in 1980 the
developed nations of North West Europe, North America, Japan and
Australasia accounted for some 67 per cent of world exports and 73 per
cent of imports by value. Using these statistics as a very broad proxy
for container potential, and making some allowance for existing penetration in developing countries, it seems that container traffic could
grow by up to about two million TEUs in the developing countries above
the 1980 level.   There might also be increasing penetration of some
large specialised cargoes; the large markets still handled by conventional refrigerated ships may present one such opportunity. After this
most of the explosive growth will have been exhausted and traffic will
move chiefly in response to growth in world trade and changes in
trading patterns.

Liner markets are unlike the tanker market where a cumulative rate of
growth in demand for transport capacity which had been sustained at
about 16 per cent per annum for decades was suddenly reduced to zero,
leaving a fleet which was in the process of doubling in size with a
tremendous shortfall of cargo. However, there could be some tendency
towards over supply as rates of growth slow down, whilst the search for
new opportunities and the desire for the growth of national fleets and

for national shipbuilding industries continue to produce increases in
capacity.

Some estimates of growth of capacity are available and are presented in
Table 2.2.

Table 2.2

Estimated Growth of Deep Sea Container Capacity 1978-84

	(Million TEUs – one way trips)
1978	10.1
1980	14.3
1982	16.1
1984	18.8

Source: World Deep Sea Container Shipping.

The figures for 1978 and 1980 were produced by a count of voyages, whilst
that for 1982 is based on NYK Line estimates of growth rates in 1981,
and that for 1984 is based on the world order book at the end of 1982,
together with estimates of the average transport capacity likely to be
provided by the new ships and of likely scrappage rates. These are
necessarily rather broad estimates, but suggest that the additional
capacity now expected by 1984 will more than cater for increasing
penetration in developing countries together with any growth that may
take place in the developed trades. Further to this the cumulative
rate of growth of some 10 per cent per annum indicated in the above
table, is much higher than that which may be expected in the deep sea
container trades once the switch to containers has been completed.

The figure of 14,300,000 TEUs can be used to derive an estimate of total
container tonnage on deep sea routes. Poor load factors and cargo
balance must account for at least 25 per cent of capacity on a world
wide basis putting the total number of loaded TEUs at no more than about
10,800,000. Taking an average of ten tonnes per TEU gives an estimate
of 108 million tonnes of cargo in 1980. [1]   So in pure tonnage terms
the deep sea container market is one of the smaller of those in maritime
transport, having only about 10 per cent of the estimated total dry cargo
movement outside of the major bulks. (Fearnley's Annual Review, 1981).

NOTES

[1]   The average weight of ten tonnes per TEU might seem rather low
      in relation to the theoretical carrying capacity of 20 tonnes for
      a 20' container and thirty tonnes for a 40' box. But the averages
      carried are much less than the maximum and 40' containers are
      limited to about 18 tonnes by road vehicle regulations in many
      countries, being used mainly for volume cargo.

3 Ship type and market role

CELLULAR CONTAINERSHIPS

The cellular system is the most efficient for moving large volumes of
containers. Cell guides provide tremendous advantages in speed and
ease of handling and as shown in Figure 3.1 they follow the shape of
the ship quite closely, maximising the container carrying capacity of
the hull. Cellular ships also provide extremely good access to cargo
which can be divided into quite small individually placed lots, and
this is an important advantage when cargo has to be segregated both by
port and weight. There are some expensive aspects of construction
because of the very open nature of the ship and the cost of the cell
guide system, but this is still the cheapest dedicated system for the
carriage of containers in large volume. It is also compatible with
very large sized ships. Indeed the technical limits have not been
reached, the constraints to ship size being in the economics and
logistics of container operations. One final feature of the system is
that most ships do not carry their own gear. This is a function of the
large size, weight and cost of shipborne cranes and the relatively poor
utilisation achieved given that ships spend only a small proportion of
their time in port.

SEMI-CONTAINERSHIPS

The market role of conventional tramps and liners was squeezed by the
development of specialised ships for bulk and semi-bulk trades on one
side and by containerships on the other. They could not match the
bulk ships for size, or the containerships for size, cargo handling
speed and levels of stevedoring costs. Nevertheless a large fleet
remains deployed in the small bulk and semi-bulk trades and on liner
routes to developing countries, and there has been a substantial design
evolution.

The earliest development was pre-container, it applied to both classes
of ship and its main features were the provision of wider hatches,
flush decks for fork lift handling in the hold and a small increase in
maximum ship size up to about 15,000 dwt. For the tween-deck tramp
this was the end of design evolution and from the mid 1960s on attention was concentrated on the large market for Liberty ship replacements
and the advantages of series production. This resulted in Austin and
Pickersgill's famous SD14 and the Spanish and Japanese Freedoms of
which some hundreds have been built. Although it went well on into the
container age this first stage of design evolution did nothing for

15

Figure 3.1

Profile and Section Drawings of the Cellular Containership Fort Royal
(31,300 dwt., 1,512 TEUs)

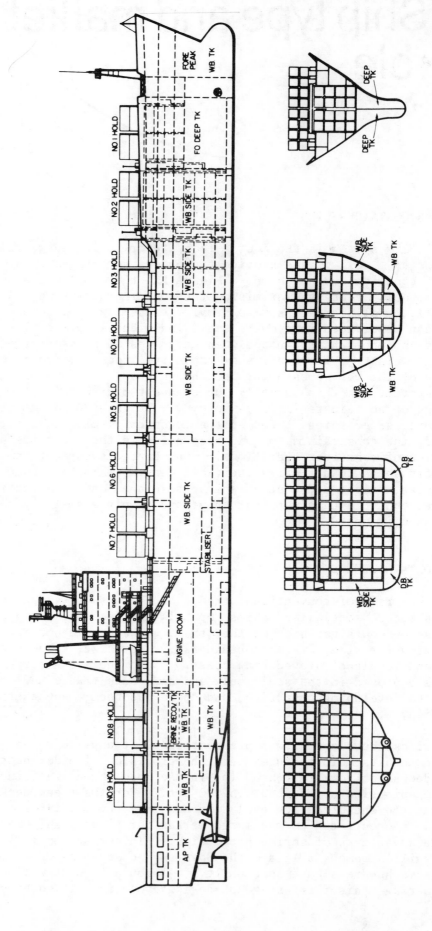

Source: The Motor Ship, November 1979.

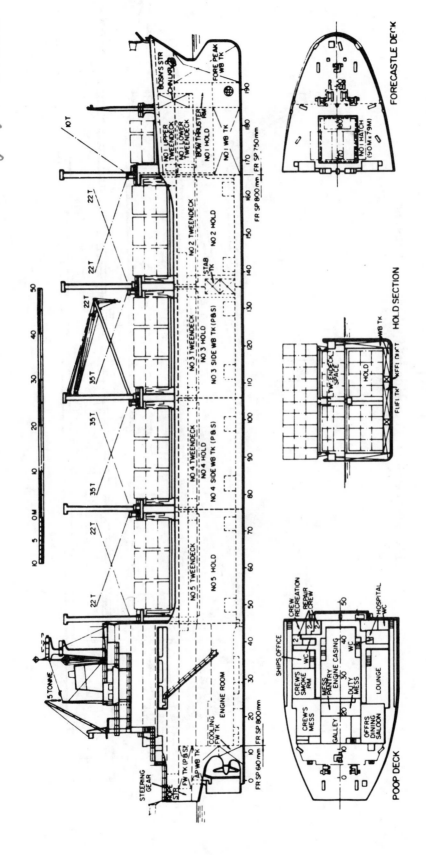

Figure 3.2

Profile and Hold Section of the Semi Containership Menelaus
(21,200 dwt., 770 TEUs)

all decks loaded up to
max 85 pct to allow
handling containers.

- have tween decks
- hatch covers (wide)
- gantry or deck cranes on board.

Source: The Motor Ship, September 1977.

Figure 3.3

Profile of the Semi Containership Corinna Drescher
(10,300 dwt., 590 TEUs)

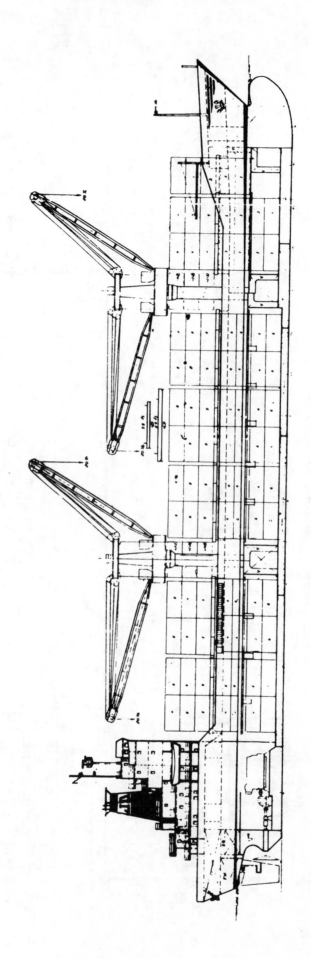

Source: Fairplay, October 1978.

container capacity, and it is difficult to carry more than about 100 TEUs on even the largest conventional ships.' This utilises only about 20 per cent of their space and weight carrying capacity and makes them quite uneconomic as container penetration increases on a route. Eventually in the late 1960s designs began to evolve again to meet the need for a container capability. Technically the problem is not too difficult; and if decks and hatches are strengthened to carry containers and dimensions, hatch sizes and deck heights are properly chosen, container capacity increases to at least 85 per cent of that of a cellular ship of the same size. The costs of doing this are not excessive and existing capacities are not impaired; but many semi-container ships were designed in the firm belief that the evolution towards containers would be slow and they only went part of the way in this development. Because of this an important opportunity was missed and some fairly new ships are unsuitable for present conditions.

The fully evolved semi-containership has moderately good container capacity, standard sized liners of 12,000 dwt. taking over 500 TEUs and a new generation of larger ships of some 20,000 dwt. approaching 800 TEUs. (On some of these ships a supplementary ro-ro ramp is added chiefly for ease of loading vehicles and wheeled equipment). At this stage the size limits of this type of design seem to be reached. The main reason is that conventional cargoes require fairly low deck heights of not more than about 18' and as ship size increases, second and possibly third intermediate tween decks are required. But it would be expensive to build a multi-deck design with all decks opening out to some 85 per cent of their area to allow for lo-lo handling and a conventional lo-lo operation would be rather cumbersome in a very big ship. Both of these difficulties can be overcome with a switch to ro-ro access where the decks are solid and high capacity tractor trailer systems can be used to move conventional and block stow cargoes.'

Even within existing design limits the semi-containership is a compromise. It has a direct cost premium over cellular ships of the same TEU capacity of some 20 per cent, this being a reflection of loss of container stowage and the cost of cargo handling gear, tween decks and more expensive hatch covers etc.' The mixed cargo handling operation also imposes problems with respect to berth procedures and manning scales and cannot really be carried out at specialised container terminals.'

DEEP SEA RO-RO SHIPS

Deep sea ro-ro ships overcome the problem of combining large size with flexible use of space and have been built in sizes up to about 2,300 TEUs. At this size the ships will carry some 700 to 800 TEUs on the weather deck in an operation which can be carried out by container gantries but could also be handled by tractor trailers and fork lift trucks over the ramp. Below the weather deck there may be three or four tween decks and in some cases car decks are also fitted. The ships can be fully self-sustaining and the ro-ro system is an economic method of achieving such a capability.' The largest jumbo ramp weighs some 350 tonnes and costs about US $1½ million, but a container gantry carried aboard a large cellular ship would also weigh around 300 tonnes and would cost about US $3 million.'

Figure 3.4

**Profile of the Deep Sea Ro-Ro Ship Nedlloyd Rouen
(25,150 dwt., 1,550 TEUs)**

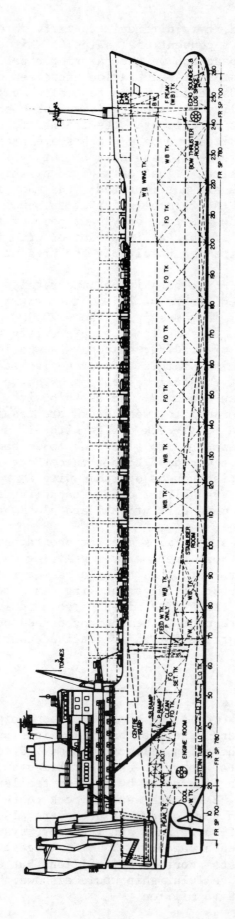

Source: The Motor Ship, July 1979.

In the early days of the container revolution the ro-ro system was put forward as a radical alternative, not just to the cellular system of container handling but to the whole container idea. This was claimed to be a result of the inherent advantages of the integrated largely horizontal nature of ship to shore transfer, contrasted with the vertical and discontinuous nature of the lo-lo operation. But although the ro-ro system does allow for more efficient handling of non-containerised cargoes it does not provide a general alternative to containerisation. In fact the system has succeeded precisely because it is compatible with containers whilst also obtaining the advantages of large size, the flexible use of much of the ships' space and a substantial capability for non-containerised cargo. However, in the handling of large volumes of containers the cellular system is acknowledged to have the edge.

CONTAINER RO-RO

Even the full ro-ro system as described above can make use of lo-lo techniques for weather deck containers. In the container/ro-ro sector this idea is carried one stage further by increasing the proportion of the ship available to lo-lo handling and in some cases even including some cellular holds in the ship. There is a range of possibilities in the way in which systems are combined. Some provide very flexible ships whilst others tend to be closely tailored to particular combinations of cargo.

Two examples of container ro-ro ships are given below. The first is of the ANRO ships which operate from Australia to Singapore. They carry containerised Australian exports northbound returning with containers plus packaged timber. The empty container problem is dealt with partly by the use of leased containers transferred from a surplus to a deficit area, and partly by the use of flat racks which can be folded for the return voyage. The second ship is a 'Sea-Containers' design. This is essentially a self-sustaining container carrying ship with a high proportion of its capacity on the weather deck. The space below the weather deck can be used for two high container stacking and with such a low stack cell guides are not required. Simple ro-ro access then allows the below deck space to be used for non-container cargoes if required.

BULK/CONTAINER SHIPS

In the bulk and semi-bulk sectors there have been various attempts to reduce the proportion of ballast steaming and provide greater trading flexibility by modifying the ships to provide capabilities outside the normal range. Most of this has been in the form of additional capabilities within the bulk sectors, but there have been some incursions into the general cargo sector and some of these have had important effects on the market as a whole.

Standard bulk carriers are in fact quite unsuitable for containers. First they are designed for slow speeds and this increases transit times particularly on the longer routes. Second they have small hatch covers designed purely for protection from the sea and this leaves a large

Figure 3.5

Profile of the Anro Class Container Ro-Ro Ships
(16,200 dwt., 955 TEUs)

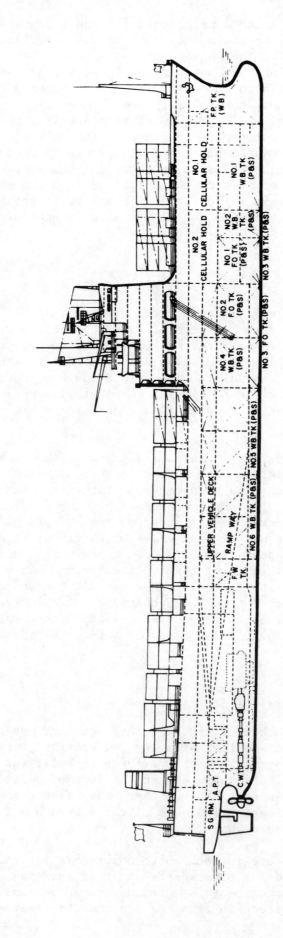

Source: The Motor Ship, November 1978.

22

Figure 3.6

Profile of the Boxer Class Container Ro-Ro Ships
(9,000 dwt., 576 TEUs)

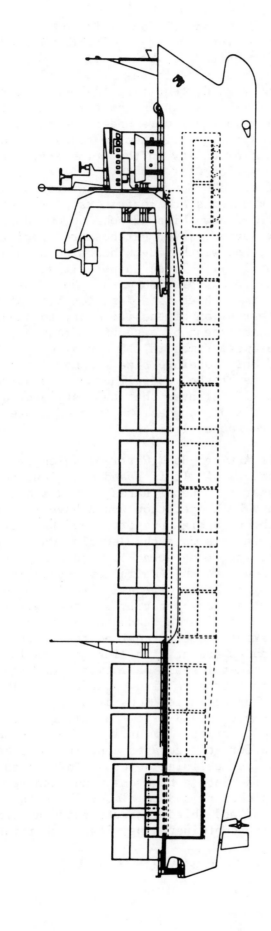

Source: Sea Containers

amount of understow in the holds as well as limiting the carrying capacity above deck to just one tier of empty or lightly loaded containers. Within the holds the tanks required to give a self trimming capacity with bulk cargoes further impede a container stow. Finally, the handling operation is very awkward, requiring the use of fork lift trucks for the outside of the holds, whilst container gantries handle only half the total capacity in the square under the hatch cover. As well as being awkward this system is limited in access to cargo and this substantially reduces flexibility in the itinerary. The main operator in recent years has been CAST who have a fleet of ships of some 40,000 dwt. operating between Montreal and Antwerp with a combination of bulk and semi-bulk cargoes and containers. Recently this company has ordered a fleet of new ships of some 60,000 dwt. in which there has been a design evolution. Two hatches are specifically designed for containers and the weather deck has also been designed for an enhanced container capability. These ships will now carry some 40,000 dwt. of bulk cargoes in association with 1,500 TEUs. They have a relatively slow transit time, which is a function both of a slow steaming speed and the interruption of the itinerary to handle bulks, but this is countered to some extent by a service frequency of five days which reduces average dwell times in the container loading ports. After being an operator of only moderate size for many years CAST are now setting out to become one of the major lines on the North Atlantic. However, the management itself believes that this style of operation requires a very particular mix of cargoes and type of route and that the opportunities world wide are rather limited.

The other major operator is Antwerp Bulk Carriers which operates a route of a totally different character. It is based on a long term contract to ship 300,000 tonnes a year of mineral sands from Western Australia to the US Gulf. A standard bulk operation would have required a return in ballast, and although a high proportion of ballast steaming is typical of bulk trades, in this case the decision was taken to use the bulk contract as the basis for an attack on the Europe Australia route and a further incursion into the Australian trades in the Pacific. In the first two ships design changes were quite small. There was some enhancement of the weather deck capacity and the hull was strengthened so that 20,000 tonnes of mineral sands could be carried in two holds without excessive flexing. This required the addition of 2,000 tonnes of steel but provided an essential element of trading flexibility as the ships pick up their mineral sands whilst on route from Europe to the major markets of Eastern Australia with containers. In the second generation there was a further evolution towards an open hatch design which increases container capacity and allows handling to be carried out entirely by shore based gantries. Finally, a third generation incorporates some 750 slots for refrigerated containers to be carried on the weather deck and in four cellular holds. This is an entirely new angle as it takes the line into a high cost and high revenue end of the market and speed has been raised to almost 18 knots to take account of this. The second and third generation are nothing like standard bulk carriers, being containerships with a subsidiary bulk capability.

Figure 3.7

General Arrangement of the Bulk Container Carrier Helen
(42,000 dwt., 1,100 TEUs)

from certain markets
return with containers

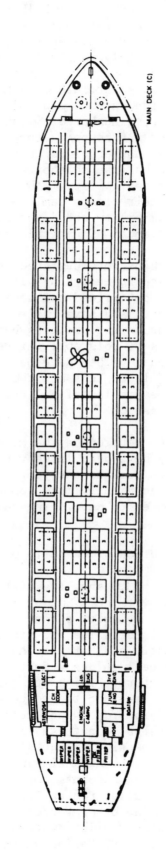

Source: The Motor Ship, December 1978.

25

SEMI/BULK SHIPS WITH CONTAINER CAPABILITY

Two main classes of semi-bulk ship with container capability are
discussed here, first, and most important the open hatch bulk carrier
and second, a specialised ro-ro design.   A ship for the semi-bulk
trades has to solve a similar problem to that of the container ship in
that cargo does not flow but has to be placed unit by unit.   Thus the
open hatch bulk carriers evolved in a similar way to container ships
with very wide hatches and holds which became smooth sided boxes.   There
are, however, a number of important differences.   First cell guides are
not required and second, since the ships operate within closed systems
to a limited number of ports in their semi-bulk trades, it becomes
feasible to utilise shipborne cranes.   These ships have a quite natural
technical compatibility with containers but they also tend to be tightly
tied into their closed semi-bulk systems.   This imposes limits on
trading flexibility and diversions into container trades which would
raise the amount of capital that has to be provided.

The ro-ro ships were designed to carry timber from the west coast of
the US to Japan, returning with vehicles and it was this latter requirement which determined the choice of handling system.   The ships are
of 42,000 dwt. and have three main decks of 6.1 metres designed specifically for forest products but also suitable for a two high container
stow.   Sets of hoistable car decks convert the ship into the vehicle
carrying mode. and They have been given a notional container carrying
capacity of 1,100 TEUs but their combined semi-bulk capability attacks
directly the problem of ballast hauls and tends to limit their interest
in containers.

A very brief mention may be made of LASH ships and other barge carriers.
So far they have been largely unsuccessful in container trades.   There
are some new designs carrying containers largely on the weather deck,
which are technically more compatible with boxes and have small shares
on some routes to developing countries.

THE DISTRIBUTION OF CAPACITY ON MAJOR ROUTES

Tables 3.1 to 3.3 show the distribution of container capacity by main
ship types over the 17 major routes in 1980 and demonstrate the pre-
dominance of cellular ships.   Some 70 per cent of total capacity was
in pure cellular ships and since most of the ro-ro capacity of the
North Atlantic and Far East Australia routes was in container/ro-ro
ships with cell guides a further 500,000 TEUs can be added to the
cellular sector, raising its share to about three quarters of the total.
Residual ro-ro capacity accounted for 12 per cent and semi and bulk
container ships for 14 per cent but these are only notional figures
since the ships do not use container capacity to the full extent.
There are some significant differences between routes.   On the three
major routes (the Atlantic and Pacific and Europe to the Far East) the
cellular system accounts for some 85 per cent of container capacity,
and in the smaller routes Europe South Africa is also predominantly
cellular.   The other routes are rather mixed, with ro-ro ships
including some trailer systems figuring strongly on those which have
short sectors, (US Caribbean and East Mediterranean to the Arabian Gulf

Figure 3.8

**Profile of the Skaugran - A Large Ro-Ro Ship for Semi Bulks
(42,000 dwt., 1,100 TEUs)**

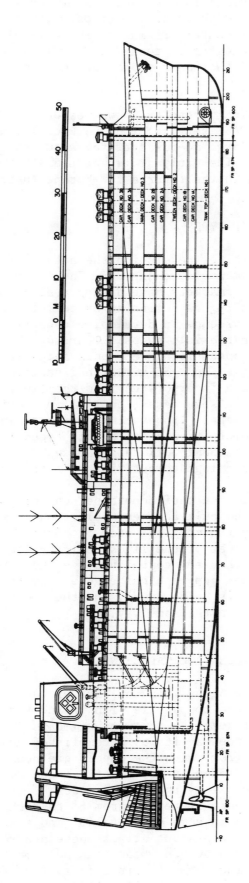

Source: The Motor Ship, May 1979.

for example) and flexible ships including semi-container systems, predominating on routes to developing countries which are still in many
cases in the process of containerising.   There is also a large ro-ro
capacity on the Europe Australia route.   This is a result of Scandinavian participation and the large proportion of semi-bulk cargoes in
the trade.

Most of the bulk container capacity shown was on the North Atlantic,
(which relates to the CAST service) and the Pacific, where open hatch
bulk carriers and the large ro-ros operate, although without carrying
very many containers.   The early stages of the ABC bulk container
service are also shown in the figures for Europe Australasia.

COMPETITION BETWEEN SHIP TYPES

As a result of the container revolution the nature of competition
between ships has fundamentally changed.   The tramps which could move
quite readily into liner markets have disappeared and on developed
routes the liner market is now dominated by cellular container ships.
A similar trend is in evidence in developing countries, although with
rather more reliance on flexible ships.   Part of the old tramp market
has been taken over by specialised semi-bulk ships (and this applies
particularly to the large flows of timber and vehicles etc.), whilst
much of the rest has been incorporated into the liner sector, either
being containerised or in some cases, carried in flexible ships in
association with containers.   However, although tramp competition has
disappeared there is competition between ship types for the medium
sized parcels of bulk and semi-bulk cargoes, and some bulk and semi-
bulk ships also provide fringe competition by carrying containers.

Since flexible ships provide their container capacity in joint supply
with other systems in the bulk and semi-bulk trades their cost structures, and particularly the marginal cost of container carrying, may
be very different from that of the lines dedicated to the container
trades.   By the same token any cost advantage that they have is
limited in its extent and geographical coverage by the nature of the
system with which there is joint supply and the amount of capacity
available is controlled in the same way.

PROSPECTS FOR FURTHER TECHNOLOGICAL CHANGE

The container revolution began when the size of cargo handling unit was
raised to the maximum size compatible with inland transport modes.
This was an increase of some ten to twenty times.   The size of the
jump was determined by the way it was accomplished, basically by taking
trucks or truck bodies from which the wheels had been removed aboard
ship;   but by this same token it left little scope for further development because limits are set by the inland modes.   It is true that
container heights have been increased from 8' to 8'6" and 9', that
length has now increased in some cases to 45' and that the weight of
a 20' box can now be 24 tonnes but all of these are relatively minor
changes.   Attempts have also been made to handle multiple units in
ship shore transfer in the form of twin lift systems for container
cranes and the use of very large trailers for ro-ro operations, but

both of these have had only limited success and application.   Ideas
have also been put forward for sectional or articulated ships in which
large blocks of containers could be handled at one time.   This has not
advanced beyond the conceptual stage, and the logistics would be very
nearly impossible on complex itineraries because the block sizes of
the discharging operation would not coincide with those of the loading
pattern.   For these reasons it is very difficult to conceive of any
revolutionary change stemming from the same source as the container
revolution viz. an increase in unit size.   In fact most of the truly
revolutionary technological change in the industry took place in the
1950s and early 1960s before containers were even introduced on to deep
sea trades.   This period saw the basic developments in containers,
ro-ro and semi-bulk systems as well as the development of ship shore
gantries, design studies for ships of up to 2,000 TEUs and the completion of the early ro-ro container designs.   Most of what has happened
since is in the form of implementation and evolutionary development,
and the scope for this is now reducing.

Table 3.1

The World-wide Distribution of Deep-sea Container Capacity in 1980

(Figures in thousands of TEU)

Trade Routes	Fully Cellular Capacity	Roll-on/ Roll-off Capacity	Semi-Container Capacity	Total capacities
1. North America - Far East	2,486	118	335	2,939
2. Europe - North America	1,838	423	451	2,712
3. Europe - Far East	1,284	33	88	1,405
4. Europe - Middle East	418	656	177	1,251
5. North America - Caribbean/ Hawaii	624	471	18	1,113
6. Europe - West Africa	152	106	305	563
7. Australasia - Far East	315	165	48	528
8. Australasia - Europe	254	82	34	370
9. Australasia - North America	207	61	86	354
10. Europe - South Africa	303	–	11	314
11. Far East - Middle East	223	57	31	311
12. North America - Middle East	91	116	78	285
13. Europe - USSR	63	160	21	244
14. Europe - Caribbean/Central America	125	20	87	232
15. North America - Central America	–	125	50	175
16. North America - South America	–	2	119	121
17. Far East - USSR	103	1	5	109
18. Far East - China	35	61	12	108
19. Other USSR trades	8	56	26	90
20. Europe - South America	14	8	68	90
21. Europe - India	4	43	39	86
22. North America - Africa	4	15	67	86
23. North America - India	–	38	36	74
24. Europe - East Africa	3	20	42	65
25. USSR - Middle East	11	38	16	65
26. Far East - Africa	5	5	50	60
27. Middle East - Australasia	35	–	8	43
28. Far East - Central America/ Caribbean	–	2	33	35
Miscellaneous	133[a]	192[b]	129	454
Totals	8,738	3,074	2,470	14,282

Notes:

a. ZIM's Mediterranean - USA - Far East service accounts for 89,000 TEU of this total.

b. Barber Blue Sea's round-the-world service accounts for 43,000 TEU of this total. As a round-the-world route comprises at least two services this figure could in fact be doubled.

Source: World Deep Sea Container Shipping.

Table 3.2

Container Capacity of Ro-Ro Ships by Route - 1980 ('000 TEUs)

Routes	Pure Ro-ro	Semi-Container Ro-ro	Container Ro-ro	Car Carrier	Heavy Lift	Hybrid Ro-ro	Passenger/ Car Ferry	Total
N. America - Far East & Japan	79,286	600	8,800	16,875	-	12,404	-	117,965
Europe - N. America	75,678	-	347,562	-	-	-	-	423,240
Europe - Far East & Japan	14,647	5,979	5,649	6,250	-	-	-	32,525
N. America - Caribbean/Hawaii	442,952	-	27,640	-	-	-	540	471,132
Europe - Middle East	571,991	5,891	70,302	1,509	216	2,552	3,624	656,085
Far East & Japan - Australia	15,642	4,752	143,583	900	-	-	-	164,877
Europe - Australia	63,713	14,950	3,195	-	-	-	-	81,857
Europe - South Africa	-	-	-	-	-	-	-	-
N. America - Australasia	61,394	-	-	-	-	-	-	61,394
Europe - West Africa	74,026	1,680	29,300	900	-	-	-	105,906
Europe - Caribbean/Central America	3,242	13,888	1,828	-	572	-	-	19,530
Far East & Japan - USSR	1,210	-	-	-	-	-	-	1,210
Far East & Japan - Middle East	13,730	-	42,933	100	-	-	-	56,763
Europe - USSR	159,689	-	-	-	-	-	-	159,689
N. America - Central America	118,868	-	6,380	-	-	-	-	125,248

Source: World Deep Sea Container Shipping

Table 3.3

Container Capacity of Semi & Bulk Containerships ('000 TEUs)

Routes	Semi-Container	Bulk Container	Total
N. America – Far East & Japan	206	129	335
Europe – N. America	174	276	451
Europe – Far East & Japan	54	34	88
N. America – Caribbean/Hawaii	16	1	18
Europe – Middle East	144	32	177
Far East & Japan – Australasia	44	5	48
Europe – Australasia	18	16	34
Europe – South Africa	9	2	11
N. America – Australasia	53	34	86
Europe – West Africa	302	3	305
Europe – Caribbean/Central America	87	–	87
Far East & Japan – USSR	4	1	5
Far East & Japan – Middle East	31	–	31
Europe – USSR	21	1	21
N. America – Central America	50	–	50

Source: World Deep Sea Container Shipping

4 Economies of scale

THE GROWTH OF SHIP SIZE AND SPEED

After the introduction of containers in 1955 the growth in ship size
was explosive.   By 1962 Sea-Land was using converted T2 tankers of
nearly 1,000 TEU capacity and by 1964 the line had completed design
studies for a fleet of cellular ships of 2,200 TEUs.   This particular
project was later abandoned, but it is remarkable that ships some five
times the size of conventional liners were under consideration before
containers had even been introduced to deep sea routes.   In the five
years between 1967 and 1972 ship size rose from a first generation of
1,000 TEUs on the North Atlantic to a second of 1,500 TEUs introduced
on the Europe Australia route and a third of 3,000 TEUs built for the
route from Europe to the Far East.   Second generation ships had speeds
of 23 knots and the Far East ships speeds of 26 knots.   They were also
twin screw ships many of which had steam turbine engines, the first of
these features carrying a fuel cost penalty of 9 per cent and the
second a penalty of about 30 per cent.   In 1972 Sea-Land introduced
the SL7s, a fleet of seven 33 knot ships of 1,968 TEUs, this being the
outcome of a parametric study in which speeds of up to 40 knots had
been considered.   A fourth generation of even larger ships was for a
time widely expected and there is no technical barrier to construction.
But by 1972 a new set of economic and operational constraints had been
reached.   The SL7s proved to be a one off case and after the fuel
price increase of 1974 high speeds, steam turbine engines and twin
screws rapidly went out of favour.

ECONOMIES OF SIZE AND SPEED

There is enormous scope for parametric variation in costs in maritime
transport systems.   They vary according to size, speed and type of
ship, the itineraries on which they are employed and handling performance in port.   Further to this the relationship between the individual
components of ship costs, capital, fuel and crew varies over time and
also in relation to flag.   Indeed one of the main features of the last
decade has been the enormous increase in relative fuel costs, whilst an
important feature of the present competitive scene is the differences
in crew costs related to flag.   In this chapter it is possible to
examine only the basic relationships and to do this on the basis of
one current set of cost structures.   The analysis is confined to
cellular containerships, which as shown above, are the predominant type
in the liner sector.   It relates to a family of ships covering a wide

range of sizes and speeds, for which basic costs at sea are shown in Table 4.1 and graphed in Figure 4.1. [1]

The analysis shows important economies of size at sea up to about 1,500 TEUs after which the curves tend to level out somewhat. This is somewhat pessimistic, as the levelling out takes place with the switch to twin engines and twin screws; the increase in capital costs and fuel consumption associated with this offsetting economies of size in an area where the slope of the curve is rather shallow. With an increase in the installed power available to a single slow speed diesel up to about 48,000 bhp., and improvements in the treatment of the hull to reduce roughness and fouling, this switch can now be avoided. Thus in their recent newbuildings American President Lines have a service speed available of 24 knots for ships of 2,400 TEUs and this would probably be possible in new built single engined ships of 3,000 TEUs. Whatever the precise speed chosen, the ability to stay within the limits of a single slow speed diesel and a single screw now means that size economies at sea continue to be significant in the larger ship sizes.

Figure 4.1 shows that there are modest diseconomies of increasing speed within the range of 19 to 23 knots, although in Figure 4.2, where some allowance is made for savings in container and inventory costs, these become insignificant. This is a rather complex subject as container and inventory costs depend upon service intervals and the precise progression of ports in the itinerary as well as ship speed, a point which will be discussed further below. Above 23 knots, increases in speed are associated with high costs, particularly when steam turbine engines are used. This factor proved to be a weakness of the large ships on the Europe Far East route leaving them vulnerable to competition from smaller and slower vessels and leading to re-engining programmes in the late 1970s and early 1980s. [2]

One of the charges frequently levelled against conference lines is that they provide excessive service quality in the form of high speeds. This is not quite the case. The tendency is to move up the speed curve in the area where the slope is rather shallow to the knee beyond which speed becomes very costly. This is to some extent a protective device because it prevents competitors from obtaining a substantial advantage in service quality for a low premium in cost. It is, therefore, a feature of competitive rather than monopolistic practice. The decision which proved most costly in recent years was the choice of steam turbines, but this was largely a technical matter in which an increase in fuel consumption was traded against greater reliability and lower maintenance costs. In the case of American lines operating under subsidy and building in domestic yards the diesel engine was not even available. Only in the case of Sea-Land was there an outright preference for high speed and even this was based on the achievement of intensive utilisation of the ship which was expected to keep total costs down to a reasonably competitive level. (Gilman, Maggs and Ryder, 1977). The main fault of the lines in this early period was that their decisions were vulnerable to fuel price increases; but so were many other decisions taken at the time, and the industry could hardly be expected to be more far seeing in respect of prospects for fuel prices than was the rest of the world.

34

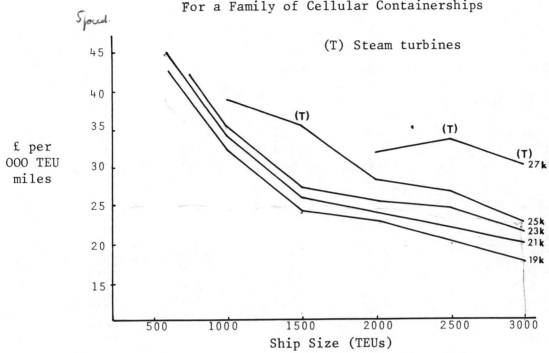

Figure 4.1

Economies of Size at Various Speeds
For a Family of Cellular Containerships

(T) Steam turbines

Spud.

£ per
OOO TEU
miles

Ship Size (TEUs)

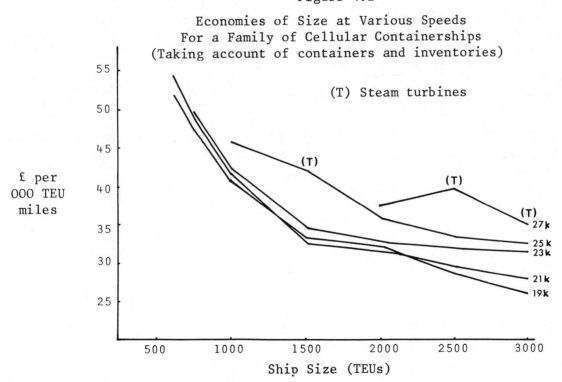

Figure 4.2

Economies of Size at Various Speeds
For a Family of Cellular Containerships
(Taking account of containers and inventories)

(T) Steam turbines

£ per
OOO TEU
miles

Ship Size (TEUs)

Table 4.1

Costs per OOO TEU Miles for a Family of Cellular Containerships

Knots	19	21	23	25	27
600 TEUs					
Fuel	18.0	20.0	-	-	-
Capital	15.8	16.4	-	-	-
I & M	3.1	3.2	-	-	-
Crew	5.9	5.4	-	-	-
TOTAL	42.8	45.0			
750 TEUs					
Fuel	16.3	18.4	20.2	-	-
Capital	15.0	15.3	14.7	-	-
I & M	2.9	3.0	2.9	-	-
Crew	4.8	4.3	3.9	-	-
TOTAL	39.0	41.0	41.7	-	-
1,000 TEUs					
Fuel	12.5	14.3	16.0	19.0	-
Capital	13.9	13.9	13.6	13.9	-
I & M	2.7	2.7	2.6	2.6	-
Crew	3.6	3.2	2.9	2.7	-
TOTAL	32.7	34.1	35.1	39.1	-
1,500 TEUs					
Fuel	8.9	10.7	12.7	20.1 (T)	-
Capital	11.7	11.6	11.2	11.6	-
I & M	2.3	2.3	2.2	2.3	-
Crew	2.4	2.1	2.0	1.8	-
TOTAL	25.3	26.7	28.1	35.8	-
2,000 TEUs					
Fuel	9.4	10.7	12.9	16.0	17.9
Capital	10.0	9.8	9.6	9.9	10.1
I & M	2.0	1.9	1.9	1.9	2.0
Crew	1.8	1.6	1.4	1.3	1.2
TOTAL	23.2	24.0	25.8	29.1	31.2

Table 4.1
(Contd.)

	19	21	23	25	27
2,500 TEUs					
Fuel	8.4	10.1	13.3	15.1	21.9
Capital	8.8	8.6	8.6	8.8	8.9
I & M	1.7	1.7	1.7	1.7	1.7
Crew	1.4	1.3	1.2	1.1	1.0
TOTAL	20.3	21.7	24.8	26.7	33.5
3,000 TEUs					
Fuel	7.4	9.4	11.2	12.7	18.4
Capital	8.0	7.8	7.8	7.9	8.1
I & M	1.6	1.5	1.5	1.5	1.6
Crew	1.2	1.1	1.0	0.9	0.8
TOTAL	18.2	19.8	21.5	23.0	28.9
Containers a)	2.9	2.6	2.4	2.2	2.0
Inventories b)	5.9	5.3	4.9	4.5	4.2
TOTAL	8.8	7.9	7.3	6.7	6.2

Source: Ship Choice in the Container Age

a)   Based on £1.3 per day for a standard 20' container.

b)   Based on an estimated £10,000 load at 10% per annum.

SHIP COSTS IN PORT

Ship costs in port behave in a totally different way from costs at sea.
Once the ship is stationary and increases in size and speed are no
longer associated with increases in transport capacity, costs increase
along both axes. It might be expected that this would be offset by
faster cargo handling for the larger ship; but this is not so and
there are diseconomies in port which are controlled by the absolute
level of cargo handling performance (which is itself a function of
container size and port efficiency) and route length. [3]   Table 4.2
takes container movement rates of 300,500 and 1,000 TEUs per day to
span the range of operational performance and computes ships costs per
TEU in port on this basis.   It shows important diseconomies in port
at the lower end of the range.   To take just one example at 300 TEUs
per day a 23 knot ship of 2,500 TEUs would have costs of £55.4 per TEU
whilst a 19 knot ship of 600 TEUs would have costs of only £24.8. The
diseconomy of size in port does of course diminish as handling rate
increases and becomes relatively unimportant at the top end of the range.

Table 4.2

Ship Costs/TEU in Port at a Range of Handling Rates (£)

	knots 19	21	23	25	27
600 TEUs					
Daily cost in Port	7,451	8,161	–	–	–
Cost/TEU 300/day	24.8	27.2	–	–	–
500/day	14.9	16.3			
1,000/day	7.4	8.2	–	–	–
750 TEUs					
Daily cost in Port	8,394	9,196	9,571	–	–
Cost/TEU 300/day	28.1	30.6	32.0	–	–
500/day	16.8	18.4	19.1	–	–
1,000/day	8.4	9.2	9.6	–	–
1,000 TEUs					
Daily cost in Port	9,856	10,657	11,223	12,211	–
Cost/TEU 300/day	32.9	35.5	37.4	40.7	–
500/day	19.7	21.3	22.4	24.4	–
1,000/day	9.9	10.7	11.2	12.2	–
1,500 TEUs					
Daily cost in Port	11,881	12,873	13,344	14,757	–
Cost/TEU 300/day	39.6	42.9	44.5	49.2	–
500/day	23.8	25.7	26.7	29.5	–
1,000/day	11.9	12.9	13.3	14.8	–
2,000 TEUs					
Daily cost in Port	13,363	14,202	15,153	16,575	18,075
Cost/TEU 300/day	44.5	47.3	50.5	55.2	60.2
500/day	26.7	28.4	30.3	33.1	36.1
1,000/day	13.4	14.2	15.2	16.6	18.1
2,500 TEUs					
Daily cost in Port	14,492	15,483	16,614	18,170	19,456
Cost/TEU 300/day	48.3	51.6	55.4	60.6	64.9
500/day	29.0	31.0	33.2	36.3	38.9
1,000/day	14.5	15.5	16.6	18.2	19.5
3,000 TEUs					
Daily cost in Port	15,577	16,566	17,981	19,441	21,281
Cost/TEU 300/day	51.9	55.2	59.9	64.8	70.9
500/day	31.1	33.1	36.0	38.9	42.5
1,000/day	15.6	16.6	18.0	19.4	21.3

Source: Ship Choice in the Container Age

Route length on deep sea routes varies from about 4,000 n.m. to 24,000 n.m. for complete round trips, each of which would have two full container exchanges, representing one container move per '000 TEU miles and one sixth of a move respectively. Size economies in these two cases are shown in Table 4.3 with the moderate container handling rate of 500 TEUs per day. Looking down the columns on the short route it is clear that size economies are virtually extinguished at about 1,500 TEUs, whilst on the longer route they continue to operate up to the Panamax size range.

SERVICE FREQUENCY AND INTEGER EFFECTS

The quality of a liner service is a function not so much of ship speed as of transit times and reliability. 'Transit times clearly depend to some extent on speed, but they are also controlled by service interval and the number of ports or trans-shipments between points of loading and discharge.' In providing a high quality service the lines tend to choose a weekly service interval. They also pay careful attention to the construction of their itineraries, trying to concentrate the discharge in the early part of their service to a particular trading area and to pick up exports in the latter part, even if this sometimes involves separate import and export calls at major ports.' The weekly service fits in with production patterns and provides a regular basis for operations, thus helping to avoid port congestion and enabling the lines to miss high cost overtime periods in certain ports. It also keeps container costs down and avoids leaving a gap in the service to shippers which could easily be exploited by a competitor.

On the shorter routes the weekly service interval has a strong effect on the operational choices available. For example on the North Atlantic the main options are for 21 and 28 day round trips for three and four fleet ships respectively. The switch to the longer round trip would provide a substantial proportional increase in the time available, particularly if it were applied just to sailing time. In this case the likely strategy is that only part of the increase would be used to reduce speed, and the rest for an extension of the route, and/or an increase in ship size. These effects also operate on longer routes although the proportional changes are less severe and more of the time can be absorbed by a reduction in sailing speed. On all routes integer effects and the need for regularity combine to reduce the flexibility with which supply may be varied, but clearly the problems are more severe on the shorter routes.

To summarise, if there is no constraint in terms of traffic it would be expected that the shorter deep sea routes would use ships of up to about 1,500 TEUs, whilst on the longer routes ships of up to 3,000 TEUs would be employed. Speeds are likely to be in the range of 19 to 23 knots although they could vary in relation to changes in the cost mix. On all routes, however, there is likely to be a range of sizes, speeds and operating patterns available depending upon the precise characteristics of the route and its traffic distributions.

Fleet sizes vary from about three to four ships typically used on the North Atlantic, up to as many as eleven on the very long routes.

Table 4.3

Ship Costs at Sea and in Port (£ per TEU)
500 TEUs per day

1,000 TEU Miles Plus One Container Move

Ship Size TEUs	Knots				
	19	21	23	25	27
600	57.7	61.3	–	–	–
1,000	52.4	55.4	57.5	63.3	–
1,500	49.1	52.4	54.8	65.3	–
2,500	49.0	52.7	58.0	63.0	72.7
3,000	49.3	52.9	57.5	61.9	71.4

1,000 TEU Miles Plus One Sixth of a Container Move

Ship Size TEUs	Knots				
600	45.3	47.7	–	–	–
1,000	36.0	37.6	38.8	42.9	–
1,500	29.3	31.0	33.5	40.7	–
2,500	24.8	26.8	30.3	32.7	39.8
3,000	23.4	25.3	27.5	29.5	35.9

SCALE EFFECTS IN OTHER SECTORS

So far the analysis has been confined to operations in the maritime sector, starting with the individual ship and going on to deal with size of fleet. But many lines operate on a wider scale than individual fleets. Some have multiple fleets, whilst others join a number of consortia, so that they have only part interests in the fleet on any particular route but operate a broad network. This raises a number of points relating to network economies, to which can be added the general question of economies of size in administrative costs and the costs of inland transport.

The advantages of a large fleet trading over several routes are that it gives the line the opportunity to provide a service of broad international coverage to large shippers, as well as providing the line itself with greater opportunities for cargo balancing and ship re-deployment. In the inland sector a larger scale of operation provides greater opportunities for inland container balancing thus helping to minimise dead heading and reduce inland costs. In some cases this can be extended to allow balancing with inland freight. In large hinterlands in particular, a competitive edge in inland transport can be very important and some of the large lines develop substantial inland transport interests to this end.

One other aspect of size economies relates to administrative functions a list of which is given below:-

Administrative Functions in Containerline Operations

Management and Operations :   Accounts
                               Booking
                               Equipment control
                               Market operations and system planning
                               Operations - ship, terminal, landside

Marketing :   Advertising, sailing schedules etc.
                               Public relations
                               Sales

Conference :   Policing

Staff requirements for such functions in a major area like the US vary between about 300 and 500 persons and the average cost per head of salaries plus social charges, pensions etc., is not less than US $24,000. Taking both ends of a route between developed areas and a minimum staffing of say 500 there would be a cost of say US $12 million per annum in salaries alone, which could easily rise to US $15 million with office accommodation and all other expenses. Some of these functions can be hived off to forwarding agents and container leasing companies, but this leads to some loss of revenue and control. To provide all of these capabilities whilst holding overheads to a reasonable proportion of freight revenues requires a certain minimum scale of operation and on the shorter routes this may be rather larger than that dictated by considerations of ship size alone. This suggests that there may be two distinct sizes of operation, one aiming at very limited sectors of the market, where the simplicity of the inland operation holds down administrative costs and the second where there is a broader higher quality service where a full administrative set up is required. The idea of a large scale operation of low overall service quality does not really make much sense, because successful operation at a large scale requires good operational control which in turn is the basis of service quality.

Finally, with the present state of the industry there are very important advantages in having strong financial backing. Many of the major container lines are supported by very powerful conglomerates and these seem to have been making quite a lot of the running in recent years.

NOTES

[1]   It is not feasible to use market prices as a basis for the study
        of the economics of ship size and speed as the market is distor-
        ted by subsidies and by inflation and covers only the limited
        range of ships under construction in a particular period.   How-
        ever, there is an alternative method available based on engineer-
        ing design studies in which ships capital costs for a large family
        of ships may be estimated on a consistent basis.   This starts
        with preliminary design studies and proceeds to estimates of steel-
        weight, wood and outfit and engines, and then by applying aver-
        age production costs to these components, and adding in the spec-
        ial items, to a total for the ship.   This approach has been used
        for the analysis, which is based on a parametric study by Burness,
        Corlett and Partners, calibrated to European prices in 1980.

[2]   Although ships may slow steam to save fuel they are still less
        efficient than when purpose built for the slower speed and there
        are certain technical disadvantages to slow steaming.

[3]   The container handling rate depends largely on the number of
        cranes which may be deployed and this is a function firstly of
        ship length and secondly of the complexity of the stow, which
        determines how much of that length can be worked at an individual
        port.   Ship length increases very much less than in proportion
        to capacity so that whilst 1,500 TEU ships are about 240m.,
        3,000 TEU ships are only some 50m., longer.   In theory this could
        mean one extra crane on the larger ship increasing the maximum
        number from four to five; but port problems relating to the
        mobilisation and distribution of cargo and the overall scale of
        operation needed to sustain a large number of cranes, tend to
        reduce the feasible maximum to three, and multi-port operations
        bring it down to two; this number being widely employed across a
        broad spectrum of ship sizes.

5 The logistics of container transport networks

CARGO DISTRIBUTION AND SHIP ITINERARIES

The basic characteristic of demand in liner shipping is that cargo distributions are dispersed, movements between port pairs being no more than moderate in proportion to service capacity, and often unbalanced. Further to this shippers and consignees require regular and frequent services limiting the period of cargo accumulation to about a week. In the conventional era there was another aspect in the form of a price structure which equalised freight rates as between ports, the effect of which was to make it necessary to call at a port in order to obtain cargo from its hinterland. The combination of these influences often resulted in extended and rather inefficient itineraries.

With the introduction of containers the problem of reaching an accommodation between cargo dispersion and scale economies was exacerbated by an increase in ship size of up to six-fold. But in the early days the idea was put forward that scale economies in container systems were such that services would consist of very concentrated trunk routes served by networks of feeders. In one extreme form this theory postulated global networks operating to no more than about five hub ports to be served by intermediate sized relays as well as feeder ships; and the hub ports were not necessarily to be located close to major cargo generating areas, ports like Falmouth being suggested for Europe and Puerto Rico for the US. There was some basis for these views. It was clearly important for container systems to escape from the extended itineraries of conventional liners, and large fast ships have to be turned round quickly to avoid size diseconomies in port. But even leaving aside the fantasies relating to world wide networks the idea of concentration never really caught on among the lines, and there is a logical flaw at the heart of it. This lies in the failure to distinguish between operational and geographical aspects of concentration. It is operational concentration only which is achieved by two port itineraries, geography is an entirely different matter.

To take just one example Sea-Land's concentrated North Atlantic itinerary with their SL7s was New York, Rotterdam and Bremerhaven, a distance of some 7,400 nautical miles. A multi-port itinerary on the North Atlantic would be likely to include one UK, one French, one Benelux and one German Port in Europe, whilst in North America it would call at New York for US imports and one or two ports in the Norfolk Baltimore range for exports. [1] This seven port itinerary is only slightly longer than the Sea-Land one and this is simply because of the extension south of New York, (the UK, French and Benelux calls being en

43

route to the German port with only relatively small diversions).
Geographical concentration or consistency is not a function of the
number of ports served, nor even of their closeness to each other but
depends on their location with respect to the main route alignment.
This in turn depends on the locations of the major cargo concentrations
on the route and their geographical relationship. Provided that ports
are on the main route alignment the extra cost of multi-port calling
will be largely that of extra port access, (including tugs and pilots
etc.), together with the extra time in port as a result of somewhat
slower cargo handling. There may be some extra distance involved but
this is not necessarily the case, and so long as the number of ports is
held within limits, cargo exchanges can still be substantially greater
than in the conventional era. Container handling costs themselves are
no greater than on concentrated itineraries and in many cases it is
easier for ports to handle a succession of moderate container exchanges
than it is for them to deal with full ship turnarounds in short periods
of high intensity working.

The other side of concentration concerns the additional costs of distribution that accrue if main line itineraries are limited. Feeder
ship and inland transport costs are much higher per TEU mile than the
costs of main line ships and additional handling costs are also substantial. To take just one illustration the feed from a Continental
port to a nearby UK port would cost not less than £100 per TEU, so that
a 200 TEU exchange (only some 6 per cent of the total of a 1,500 TEU
ship), would cost about £20,000 - equivalent to two additional days in
port. With the SL7s Sea-Land operated a 14 day itinerary at about 28
knots, whilst the other lines were operating 21 day round trips at 23
knots. These alternatives were compared in a parametric study at 1977
prices and it was found that the basic ship costs of the two systems
were roughly the same so that the broader distribution of the multi-port
service was a clear benefit. (In this respect it may be noted that
although a concentrated itinerary gives faster transit times between the
base ports, the differences are only small whilst trans-shipment involves substantial additions to transit times).

A few lines tried to follow the ideas of concentration to the letter
although even in these cases route networks eventually evolved to
encompass multi-port operations with quite large ships. However, most
lines were rather more pragmatic. There was amalgamation of services
to obtain adequate scale and this led to the formation of new operating
consortia. New route structures were then developed, which although
they did not go to the extremes of concentration, were still substantially rationalised compared to conventional operations. Certainly
the combination of container technology and new route structures led to
a quantum reduction in the number of ships employed. Main line services could also be linked to give greater breadth without excessive
complication of mother ship itineraries and these basic networks could
be supplemented by the use of inland transport and feeder ships.

INTER-MODAL TRANSPORT AND NETWORK EXTENSION

Two of the particular features of container systems are the ease of
trans-shipment and the ability to make extensive use of inland modes.
There was some trans-shipment in the conventional system, but it carried

high risks of damage, delay and loss and was generally avoided. With containers these dangers are much reduced and although there is still some shipper preference for direct routes, this does not prevent the development of complex patterns including the inter-linking of main line ships and the use of feeders. The increased use of inland modes is only partly a function of containerisation and ease of inter-modal transfer as it has also depended on the general evolution of these modes and particularly the development of the motorways and of unit trains. It is arguably a more important development than trans-shipment, part-icularly when the use of overland routes makes available substantial savings in distance. New route patterns then become available, many of them utilising land bridges of various types. [2]

The US provides a number of mini bridge possibilities. The most impor-tant is probably that of US routes linking east coast hinterlands to the Far East. The all water route from New York to Japan via Panama is some 11,500n.m. whilst the land route via San Francisco is only 7,750n.m. For mid west cargoes the balance in favour of the west coast route is obviously improved. A similar logic applies to west coast markets to Europe which can shorten the land leg by using Gulf ports instead of those in the New York - Cape Hatteras range. Even on the north south axis there are cases where a switch of routes will allow a small increase in inland miles to provide substantial savings in sail-ing distance. This applies for example to mid west cargo for South America, which can move south to Miami or other Gulf ports, forsaking traditional east coast outlets. Turning to other areas the Trans-Siberian Railway shortens distances between Europe and the Far East, and has in recent years taken up to 10 per cent of traffic. In routes between Europe and the Middle East, land and mini bridges offer quite substantial savings in distance; and for all deep sea routes tran-sitting the Mediterranean, mini bridges based on South European ports offer savings in distance for most Continental European cargoes. Savings in distance do not provide a prima facia case for the use of a land or mini bridge route. Sea transport is very substantially cheaper than the land modes per tonne mile and has the advantage that it requi-res no track. So even quite substantial savings in distance from the use of a land or mini bridge could prove insufficient to make it comp-etitive on a straight cost basis. But there are two other aspects, the first being that ship costs are indivisible whilst inland costs can be tailored to quite small numbers of boxes and the second that the trade flow may be unbalanced whilst the use of an inland mode may allow balancing to take place with inland freight. Where these factors in favour of inland modes can work together, land and mini bridge options become much more attractive. They can be based on full cost pricing, (i.e. bearing the full cost of inland transport and paying the relevant conference rate on the marine sectors), but as competition develops it can also lead to price wars. These may be between conferences and the outsiders who could be expected to search out new route patterns, or there may be inter conference competition as inter modalism tends increasingly to allow encroachment across traditional boundaries. New pricing structures for inland transport facilitate these developments.

In the conventional system freight rates were quoted 'ship's rail to ship's rail' and although there was great scope for variation by commodity, they were usually equalised as between the major ports served. Indeed it was this commonality of rate structure by port which defined

the conference boundaries.   In this system shippers and consignees
minimise their total freight costs by minimising the variable inland
component of the freight.   In some cases where potential competition
between conferences arose this would be countered by adjustment of the
level of conference rates and there were also cases where ports and
inland modes, particularly the railways, worked together to sustain
established patterns.   Thus ports tended to have fairly well defined
and stable hinterlands which usually encompassed most of the local area,
and in spite of the power of conferences the choice of port lay with
shippers and consignees.   A conventional pricing structure does not
prevent lines from trading broadly across the conference area but it
does limit them to the use of direct calls or feeder services, (which
bear the same freight as direct calls as the line is allowed to absorb
feeder ship costs) and this is an important constraint.   With inter-
modal or door to door pricing the costs of inland transport can be
absorbed to some extent so that the shipper pays the same rate irrespective of the choice of port.   This makes shippers and consignees
much less concerned with choice of port or even completely indifferent
to it and brings inland modes into transport networks in a much more
substantial way.   Systems of absorption pricing, based on 10 km. inland
grids, were developed first by the UK Australia conference as the lines
set out to rationalise their calls on a European basis, limiting the
number of UK calls.   They were designed to maintain the equity of the
system as it affected shippers remote from the single port chosen and
also to close the door to prospective competition which might otherwise
exploit inland rate differentials.   A similar system was taken up by
the UK North Atlantic conference but this was a means of ending a fierce
rate war which developed as lines set out to widen their markets.

It is now possible to consider the general character of container transport networks.   At the centre will be main line itineraries, which will
be geographically consistent but may nevertheless contain a number of
ports.   These may be linked at various points to allow for broader
overall coverage.   Individual ports within the main line itineraries
can then serve as centres for feeder ships or termini for long overland
routes, the choice of port depending on transport geography but also to
some extent on historically established patterns and political links.
In some cases, however, the use of inland modes in land and mini bridge
routes allows for the establishment of radically new transport patterns.
Coming back to our European example a single UK port located in the
south east can serve the whole of the country by the extensive use of
inland modes, with a supplementary feeder service for Irish traffic; a
German port can serve as a base for a feeder service from the whole of
Scandinavia whilst the UK and French ports can handle feeder services
from the Iberian Peninsular, the Mediterranean and Africa.   Finally
Continental ports can take rail services from central and eastern
Europe and some areas in the Mediterranean region.

As a result of the development of container networks competitive patterns
are very substantially altered.   First there can be greater competition
within conferences, closed or open, simply because of the increased size
of ship and the wider catchment areas served by individual ports.
Depending upon the geography of the trading area there can also be
greater competition between conferences by the use of feeder services,
main line interchanges, land and mini bridge routes.   As a result some
conference lines are carrying large quantities of non conference cargo

from outside the conference area.   Non vessel operating common
carriers can also be active in putting together new competitive route-
ings.   Finally, there are cases where the land modes substitute for
most of the maritime route as with the Trans Siberian Railway.

Even in the conventional era shipping services were often broader than
individual conference boundaries.   With modern networks the disparity
becomes even greater and on any given route lines are often members of
many conferences.   So although on some routes the conference may coincide with the service, and in principle be a rationalising body, on
other routes it is not, and capacity rationalisation requires associations of conferences.   Even then lines and operating consortia would
often be taking conference decisions as an input to their own wider
networks.

PARAMETERS OF NETWORK DESIGN

In the construction of networks lines will usually look at sets of
total costs for the alternatives under consideration rather than use an
analytical approach comparing the individual components of these alternatives.   But there is some value in identifying the parameters controlling the outcome of such comparisons and considering individual
trade offs and inter-relationships.   In particular this can help in
understanding the character of trading hinterlands and the logic of
container line networks.   The main parameters, which have already been
discussed in general terms above, are cost differentials between marine
and inland modes, geographical ratios between marine and inland distances, cargo distribution and pricing structures, and regulatory policy.

Cost Ratios and Cargo Proportions

The basic cost ratios are shown in Table 5.1 below.   Since ship costs
are indivisible (whereas inland costs can be tailored quite closely to
inland modes) they are modified according to load factor.

Table 5.1

Mother or Feeder Ship Costs (£)

Ship Size TEUs	Speed Knots	Cost per Day at Sea	Cost per '00 TEU mile Load Factor %			
			100	50	25	10
200	13	3,207	5.14	10.28	20.56	51.4
600	19	11,760	4.28	8.56	17.12	42.8
1,000	19	14,940	3.27	6.54	13.08	32.7
1,500	21	20,360	2.67	5.34	10.68	26.7
3,000	23	29,990	2.15	4.30	8.60	21.5

Plus £3,000 to £8,000 for port access

N.B.   In the inland sector road costs are about £75 per 100 TEU miles
and rail costs are £50 per trip plus £30 per 100 TEU miles.

The table shows that in terms of straight costs per TEU mile, sea transport is very competitive with the inland modes, being only one thirtieth of the cost when a 3,000 TEU ship at full load is being compared with road transport. However, if the ship requires a special diversion from its main route alignment and only a small proportion of its cargo is involved the difference can be substantially narrowed. Port access costs can also become very important when only small quantities of cargo are involved.

Convexity Ratio

The convexity ratios measure the differences in distance travelled between competing maritime and inland modes. Where the maritime distance is less than the land distance this merely supports the natural use of the sea. However, there are many cases where the use of a land or mini bridge will allow a short cut to be taken and in some of these the ratio of maritime distance saved to increased inland distance can be very high. This can be a powerful factor in helping to offset the natural advantage of sea transport.

Cargo Balance Factor

This ratio expresses the differences in load factor which will be achieved by inland modes on land or mini bridge routes and those which will be obtainable in direct ship services.

Pricing Structures

With conventional or full cost pricing for inland transport, competition within and between conferences is limited by shipper and consignee choice of local ports and the need to serve these ports in order to obtain cargo. Inter-modal or absorption pricing systems for inland transport allow lines to collect freight from far off hinterlands by inland mode and develop their networks using cost minimisation techniques. This can also open the door to a form of marginal cost pricing in which the inland rather than the sea freight is reduced.

NOTES

[1]   Non US lines have to operate multi-port itineraries as inland freight rates tend to sustain established hinterlands and the Jones Act prevents them from operating coastal services.

[2]   A pure land bridge occurs when an all water route is replaced by a shorter route with a central land section e.g., Europe to the Far East westbound via a land link in the US rather than the Panama Canal. Mini bridges occur when an existing route between two trading hinterlands is replaced by a shorter one which goes overland to a new port.

6 Classical models of conference behaviour

The last four chapters have been concerned with the detailed structure of supply and demand in the container shipping industry and will be used to help develop a general view of its competitive dynamics. Before going on to this there are two aspects of the traditional approach towards conferences which must be dealt with. The first of these is concerned with the use made of neo classical models of monopolistic competition to explain and evaluate conference behaviour, and the second with differential pricing structures.

THE CLASSICAL MODEL

Concentration of market power has always been regarded with distrust and there has been legislation against monopolies since the late 19th century. But an accepted theoretical formulation of the operation of monopolistic markets had to wait until the publication of works by E.H. Chamberlin and Joan Robinson in the late 1940s. Certain aspects of this theory have been applied to liner shipping markets and this has led to an interpretation of their functioning which places great stress on the differences between types of conference to the relative exclusion of other factors.

The lead is taken from that part of Chamberlin's work which deals with an oligopolistic market in which price maintenance is associated with free entry. He believed that this would lead to excess capacity for which there was no automatic corrective (a view based on his proposition that in a monopolistic market, where firms set prices so that marginal revenue equals marginal cost, they will earn greater than normal profits). The position can be maintained indefinitely if there are effective barriers to entry, but without such barriers new firms enter the market, reducing the output of all, increasing costs per unit and bringing profits back to normal. Much of the work on liner markets has been based on this original perception. Thus Devanney postulated a situation in which companies in an open conference, finding themselves in a situation of over capacity would raise prices to a satisfactory level, following which there would be further tendencies towards over capacity, the process being likened to a ratchet which allows movement only in one direction. He also believed that there would be a tendency to excessive service competition and fragmentation in operations and suggested that there was evidence of this in conventional operations; although the alternatives he suggested to make this case were wildly unrealistic. Davies started with specific reference to Chamberlin's model and then suggested additional mechanisms by which

49

decision making within open conferences would lead towards over capacity, arguing that closed conferences could avoid this problem by controlling their own capacity and deterring entry with the threat of rate wars.

One of the most interesting approaches towards the COAR system was that of Deakin, who considered the application to it of the public utility standards usually reserved for industries where capacity and rate making is much more tightly regulated than in liner shipping. Deakin accepted that freight rates should be based on externally validated voyage accounts but suggested that where there was variation between lines, any increase in rates should be less than the average of cost increases. He also believed that means should be available whereby the more efficient low cost operations within the conference could increase their share at the expense of the less efficient. Provided that these conditions were met Deakin believed that conferences would meet five out of seven economic standards laid down by Baumol for public utilities and could be accepted as operating broadly in the public good. These were the prevention of monopoly profit; the provision of a strong motivation for operating profit and innovation; the prevention of predatory competition against outsiders; the elimination of the motive for uneconomic investment as a means of expanding the rate base and avoidance of other socially undesirable means of expanding the rate base. The two rules not met related to administratively determined rates the burden of which would fall on those shippers whose demand was relatively inelastic. Deakin recommended that if conference profitability could be improved an effort should be made to reduce cross subsidy and value relating pricing and satisfy the remaining standards. This approach is a consistent one based firmly on theories of monopolistic competition. But even if this argument is accepted there would be serious problems in implementation. First on the smaller routes there may be only one consortium, so that internal competition and adjustment of market share could not take place. Second even in the large markets it would hardly be likely that the lines would allow changes in market share to be imposed on the basis of estimates of relative costs, and arguments about the true meaning of costs and relative operational efficiency would be divisive and ultimately inconclusive. Baumol's provisions have never been taken on board in the formulation of Codes of Conduct for liner conferences and the guarantees that Deakin said were needed are not really available in a truly monopolistic market. In such a market rates can be kept in line with costs by monitoring arrangements, but overall efficiency depends upon the accuracy of the economic and operational judgements of the monopolist and his willingness to make adjustments when required without external pressures.

This brief review can not do justice to the extensive literature on conferences, but it is clear that there is a broad body of opinion which considers that if there has to be a degree of monopoly power, this can only be justified if the conference system is closed and rationalised, any counter weight being provided by Shippers' Councils. The open conference system receives little support and is usually regarded as the worst of all possible worlds and probably the cause of over capacity. In the mid 1970s the evidence might have appeared to support such an interpretation. Three of the best known closed conference routes, those from North West Europe to the Far East, South Africa and Australasia were behaving as rationalised systems should, whilst the North Atlantic as a large open conference route was clearly rather messy and volatile and had been subject to overtonnaging and rate wars.   But in recent years some closed conferences have had serious difficulties and this leads one to question the classical interpretation of market function.

Once challenged it does seem that the classical models take a rather simple and mechanistic view of the operation of liner markets, and give no place at all to basic influences affecting supply and demand.   There clearly are such factors, as changes in the rate of growth of demand along the 'S' curve of container penetration and changes in cargo balance brought about by exchange rate variation are quite difficult to accommodate, whilst on the supply side there are tendencies towards over capacity stemming from the support of shipping lines and shipbuilding on non commercial principles.   The analysis of earlier chapters can also be applied to markets, showing that they vary greatly in their competitive character;   and any appreciation of the relative effectiveness of the varying forms of conference organisation should take this into account.   Finally the classification of conferences simply in terms of the open or closed nature of their membership may be criticised as too simple.   For example some conference systems (like that provided for by the UNCTAD Code) may have cargo sharing provisions substantially affecting their operation.   The strength of tying arrangements with shippers also varies depending upon the precise nature of the contract. For all these reasons the mechanistic view of liner markets needs to be replaced with a broader interpretation.

DIFFERENTIAL PRICING

The models of market function criticised above employ a general concept of the average level of conference freight rates.   But rate structures are in reality very complicated and a great deal of work has been done to understand their rationale and explain their economic consequences. This will be briefly reviewed, but most of the work has been done on conventional rates and some thought will also be given to the changes resulting from containerisation.

Conventional Rate Structures

Studies of the structure of freight rates have explored their relationship to a number of variables.   On the cost side these include the stowage characteristics of the cargo, consignment size, handling rates, priorities and the special costs incurred in the handling of refrigerated and hazardous cargoes.   On the demand side the value of cargo is taken into account and attention is also paid to competition from tramp and semi bulk ships.   Finally, there are archaic elements and inconsistencies within rate structures which add to the difficulty of explanation.

In order to examine statistically this multi causal structure of rates multiple regression techniques are required, and these have been applied by a number of economists starting with Heaver and including Bryan and Schneerson.   The most comprehensive attempt, however, was by Deakin and Seward who based their investigation on 4,300 consignments carried in four conventional ships and one container ship in 1970.   The model took stowage rate as a basic factor (expressing rates in relation to freight tonnes) and the explanatory variables then included the special costs of carrying hazardous and refrigerated and cooled cargoes, as well as value of the goods shipped and consignment size.   The results were tentatively presented, but in so far as the model could explain the price structure, cost based factors gave one third of the explanation and demand factors (i.e. the value of the goods shipped) the remaining two thirds.   But the relationship was a very subdued one, freight rates increasing only in line with log e of the value of the goods. This result has been confirmed in other investigations and since freight rates on most routes have a range of only about three to one whilst the value of goods can vary enormously, it is clearly of general validity.   Deakin and Seward criticised what they took to be value of service element in pricing, but found that high value goods cross subsidised the low ones so that there was a welfare transfer rather than the extraction of monopoly profits.

The value related interpretation of differential rate structures can be criticised on two main grounds, the first related to cost differences associated with value, and the second to the assumed relationship between value and the elasticity of demand.   A set of cost related reasons why lower value goods should have lower freight rates were identified by Evans.   These included the following :-

(a)   That they were required for the stability of
        the vessel or could be stowed in spaces
        unsuitable for other cargoes.

(b)   That they did not require expensive tween deck
        space or the care of some high value cargoes.

(c)   They were carried at lower priorities than high
        value cargoes and could be used to relieve
        seasonal peaks.

(d)   They allowed an increase in vessel size and a
        reduction in long run marginal costs.

(e)   They did not require the high quality service
        of other liner cargoes and had to be priced at
        rates close to those of competing tramp ships.

Evans also argued that the differential rate structure was formed by the operation of natural competitive forces, and where low rates encouraged the movement of cargoes on 'thin' legs there was no cross subsidisation, but rather a contribution from the lower rated goods which would keep prices down on the rest.

Schneerson's model included cargo handling rates as one of the explanatory variables.   The results have been criticised as unrealistic but he raises an important point.   Typically in the conventional era high value liner cargoes could be handled at only about seven tonnes per gang hour whilst the lower value and more homogeneous semi bulk cargoes could be handled at twenty five tonnes per hour.   This allows a significant reduction in cargo handling cost, (part of which is included in the sea freight rate) and it also means that the semi bulk cargoes needed relatively less ship time in port.   Indeed if the semi bulk cargo could be handled in several hatches simultaneously, whilst the smaller parcels of liner cargo were handled in only one or two hatches at a time, this difference could be substantial.

Turning to the demand side the basic explanation of the relationship between price and value arose from consideration of the derived nature of the demand for sea freight. The characteristics of derived demand were investigated by Walters and Bennathan applying the basic formula set out in Marshall's Principles. This was as follows:

| The derived elasticity of demand for transport | = | transport cost as a fraction of final price | x | elasticity of demand for good |

Concentration on the second term of this equation (with the general presumption of a neutral third term) leads to the expectation that the elasticity of demand for transport will reduce as the value of the goods shipped increases and that this allows higher freight rates. But if attention is focussed on the third term this presumption must be modified. Some of the commodities which move in liner services are semi-processed goods or intermediate manufactures which often form only a very small component in the final price of the article sold to the consumer. This may apply to the timber used in house building, or motor car components, to take just two simple examples. In these cases the demand for the goods in question may be almost totally insensitive to movements in the sea freight rate. But many such goods may be supplied from a variety of sources and it is possible that a reduction in the sea freight rate would allow substitution to take place between competing suppliers, in which case the change in quantity shipped could be substantial. Similarly some products might be shipped in semi bulk ships and may switch to liners if the rate drops to a competitive level, this change also being completely unrelated to the total quantity consumed. Thus it cannot be assumed that in general low value goods will have a higher response to given freight rate changes than high value goods. They may be quite insensitive to price over a large range but move significantly if it drops to the level where substitution takes place. High value goods vary enormously in character and no generalisation can be made about derived elasticities. But if changes in freight rate are of short term duration they will often be absorbed by distributors and have no effect on market prices.

There is another more general point which is that there can be a great deal of movement in the background conditions controlling the development and pattern of international trade and this could swamp the effect of changes in freight rates or at the very least make them very difficult to detect. Among long term changes in trading patterns reference can be made to the growth of Japan and the newly industrialising countries of the Far East which have become major generators of cargo, the enormous increase in the imports in OPEC countries in the mid and late 1970s following increases in oil prices, and entry of the UK into the European Economic Community, which favoured short sea trades to the detriment of deep sea trades. Among shorter term movements are those caused by changes in currency values, which in the era of flexible exchange rates can alter the relative prices of a country's exports by as much as 25 per cent within a year. This affects trade not just because of the elasticity of demand in the consuming market but also because it affects the shares of individual suppliers. (The effect of exchange rate variation is of course modified by differences in domestic inflation rates.) Changes of substantial magnitude can also occur in prices of those agricultural commodities which fall within the general cargo sector, coffee, wool and copper, to name just a few examples, although these often happen in response to climatic factors. For all of these reasons changes in ocean freight rates have limited effects on the volume of cargo moving in liner trades, so that when there is over supply most of the re-adjustment must take place in terms of reduced load factors and/or the eventual withdrawal of capacity from the market. For these reasons rate wars tend to be severe.

The Effect of Containerisation

Containerisation revolutionised cost structures within the liner shipping industry and also changed the balance of cargoes carried so that a new set of influences became important. Light cargoes became of particular significance as they allow the use of the upper tiers of the weather deck of a containership, where even cargoes of moderate weight would often cause stability problems. Second, containers need to be kept in balance, and the cost of providing services to individual shippers and consignees depends very much on the pattern of inland movements in the network as a whole as this determines the cost of placing containers at the loading point. The use of special containers exacerbates this problem as they often have to be returned empty or at least have long balancing moves between delivery to the consignee and arrival at the next shipper. Container balancing costs cannot always be passed on as they run counter to shippers' views on equity, and for this reason they often have to be absorbed within the sea freight rate. Since they are a function of the configuration of individual networks they will also vary considerably between lines in a non systematic way.

Refrigerated and hazardous cargoes still carry their high cost and where hazardous cargoes require a special ship call the delay to the ship can be particularly costly. There are also differences in cargo handling rates related to size of container and the effects that particular consignments have on the complexity of the stow and the structure of the itinerary. Finally, there is the question of ship size and the greater spread of sizes between routes. Other things being equal marginal costs on the long routes will be lower than on short routes, allowing a greater differential in freight rates to encourage movement of cargo. Although cost structures were revolutionised by containerisation rate structures did not at first change very much. Indeed when introducing containers the general policy was to maintain the general level and structure of conventional rates and to provide benefits to shippers chiefly in the form of improvements in service quality, specifically faster transit times and reductions in pilferage and damage. However, as time has gone on there have been substantial changes. A very complex analysis would be required to establish the precise variables which now control freight rates and to measure their effect. However, as a general proposition it seems unlikely that there is any very strong element of value related pricing left on any routes which have been subject to strong competition in recent years. A second point which bears more directly on future conference action is that variety in network costs provides greater incentives to follow an independent pricing policy than existed in the conventional era.

7 Market function in the intermodal age

In moving towards a more realistic analysis of the workings of container shipping markets it is necessary to blend the results of the earlier chapters on the structure of supply and demand with an understanding of the way in which shipping lines co-operate and compete with each other.   In this it is possible to draw on some of the concepts used in marketing and particularly on the idea of market share.

Most companies operating in an oligopolistic market are likely to have accurate ideas of its size and rate of growth as well as estimates of future growth.   They will know their own market share and quite possibly will know or have estimates of the market shares of their competitors.   Finally, they will have some knowledge of the strengths, weaknesses and styles of operation of their competitors and may have a shrewd idea of their likely responses to developments in the market. The formulation of policies usually focuses around estimates of market share, which are used in the preparation of estimates of costs and revenues.   Governments also formulate their policies in relation to the share of national lines in domestically generated trade.   The following section examines the way in which the characteristics of supply and demand determine the options available to lines with respect to market share.   Following this some thought will be given to the competitive strategies of outsiders and conferences and to scenarios for routes of various types.

ROUTE SIZE, SCALE ECONOMIES AND MARKET SHARE

The unit of production in the container shipping industry is the fleet capable of providing a weekly service.   With large ships this gives a capacity of some 300,000 TEUs per annum and with medium sized ships it is about half of this.   When these figures are set alongside those of capacities on world routes it can be seen that there are only a few of them which will sustain more than one or two dedicated services of full scale.   The two largest trade routes are the Pacific and the Atlantic, both of which employ ships which are predominantly in the medium size range and have a capacity equivalent to twenty services with ships of this size.   The route from Europe to the Far East has a much lower traffic density and can employ the very largest containerships, at which size it would sustain five weekly services.   There is only one other trade route in this league, that from Europe to the Middle East, but this is very fragmented, with origins from the Baltic to the

Adriatic and destinations from the Eastern Mediterranean to the Arabian Gulf, giving great variation in route length and freight rates. Leaving this and the relatively short route from the US mainland to Puerto Rico aside, the next largest routes are from the Far East to Australasia and Europe to West Africa, both roughly in the region of 550,000 TEUs per annum. Two of the classic COAR routes, Europe to Australasia and South Africa are shown to be relatively small with some 370,000 TEUs and 314,000 TEUs capacity respectively in 1980.

Route size in relation to size economies is the prime factor in determining competitive character. Only on the two largest routes in the world is it possible to contemplate a weekly service with medium sized ships and still be aiming at only a moderate share of the market, and one which might in principle be accommodated by growth over two to three years. Even on the Far East route the market share with 1,500 TEU ships would be over 10 per cent, and with the most economic Panamax sized ships over 20 per cent. Australasia and North West Europe to South Africa both require only one or at most two weekly services.

Competition at Less Than Full Scale

Trans-shipment and the use of land and mini bridges allow competition on the basis of joint supply and at a scale which is much less than that of dedicated container services. This was described in Chapter 5, where it was shown that the opportunities depend very much on the geography of the route. The routes from North West Europe to Australasia and South Africa are relatively isolated from competition of this type, whilst that from North West Europe to the Far East and many of the routes in the USA face severe land and mini bridge competition.

The capabilities of flexible ships were described in Chapter 3. As in the case of inter modal competition the opportunities depend very much on the nature of the route, although in this case it is the nature of the cargo flows rather than geography which is the crucial feature.

Flag Shares and Cargo Generation

One of the important aspects of liner shipping in the modern world is the aspiration for national fleets and the tendency to relate the carryings of these fleets to domestic cargo generation. This finds its clearest expression in the UN Code of Conduct, but it is also in evidence in established shipping nations concerned over the share of domestic lines, and in some countries with traditionally rather smaller interests in shipping such as Australia and Canada. As a result of these influences the greater the number of trading partners on a route and the greater the disparity between cargo generation and the market shares of national lines the greater will be the potential for competition. As an example one can contrast the N.W. Europe Far East route which has many trading nations, some of which have small shares in relation to the cargo they generate, with the N.W. Europe South Africa route, where there is a limited number of participants and shares reflect cargo generation. When considering this aspect one must take particular account of the newly industrialising countries and particularly those of the Far East. Competition from these countries is strong in shipping, as in many other areas of industrial

activity.   Two of the five large container routes of the world are
with the countries of the Far East as well as a number of secondary
routes.   On all of these there is strong competition from the shipping
lines of the n.i.c.s.

Changes in the Cost Mix

There have been very substantial changes in the balance of ship operating costs in the last two decades, as can be seen from Table 7.1.

Table 7.1

Rates of Escalation of Ship Capital and Operating Costs (% Increase)

	1960s	1970s
Ship Capital Costs	5.0	9.0
Maintenance	6.0	11.0
Crew Costs	7.0	12.0
Fuel Costs	0.0	25.0

The main element in this table is the decline in relative fuel costs in
the 1960s, followed by the tremendous increase in the mid and late
1970s.

All the early decisions on containership design were taken at a time of
low fuel costs which were declining in relative terms.   As a result of
this many lines were caught out in choice of speed and engine type,
this factor providing opportunities for newcomers in the mid and late
1970s.

Finance is a significant element in the cost mix, first because of its
direct effects and secondly because easy terms increase the ease of
entry.   In recent years of over capacity in world shipbuilding some
lines have been able to obtain ships for very low down payments with
extended repayment terms and easy credit.

COMPETITIVE STRATEGIES

The question of competitive strategy can be approached by considering
the options of new entrants on routes of various types.   Referring
first to the smaller routes it is clear that any attempt to run a
dedicated service at full scale on a route already provided for would
lead to a catastrophic all round drop in load factors.   On many routes
such a move would be prevented by government support of national lines,
but even where this does not apply it is clearly a strategy which would
be bound to result in a fierce competitive battle and could succeed
only if the existing lines were displaced from the market.   This might
be feasible if the new line had a powerful new technology on its side
as was the case for some of the early container operators.   Otherwise
the most likely form of competition on small routes would be from
fringe operators using flexible ships, trans-shipment or land bridges
etc.   They would offer a lower quality of service than the conference
lines and operate as outsiders using price discounts to obtain traffic.

On large routes there is also likely to be competition from fringe operators as described above. This will apply to open and closed conference routes alike, but although there are substantial price discounts, fringe operators have neither the service nor the capacity to mount a serious attack on the conference. This leaves the question of the larger lines capable of providing a high quality of service by themselves. One of the features of competition from such lines on the open conference routes, which at first sight seems paradoxical, is that many of them prefer to operate as outsiders. On closer examination, however, it is seen that there are many advantages in the use of an outsider strategy. There is only one advantage for a new entrant in taking conference membership, which is that if he supplies only part of a shippers' needs there is no loss of discount to the shipper on the rest of his cargo shipped with the conference. But this is only of value to a line contemplating a weak marketing strategy where it is prepared to share most of its customers. By itself open conference membership offers neither a guaranteed share of revenues nor an uncontested slot in the service pattern, and there are also some important costs associated with it. For a line with an established marketing network in the hinterlands served, conference membership might be a feasible method of entry, but without these advantages it is not. Thus an outsider strategy in which price competition is the essential element is often the preferred method of entry.

On the shorter routes this approach is facilitated by the fact that only three or four ships are required to offer a weekly frequency. Service oriented outsiders may go further than this and offer multiple services of broad geographical coverage so that they match the breadth of the conference in covering the shippers' needs. One example is that of Trans Freight Lines on the North Atlantic who built up to three services, although with ships of only moderate size. Where outsiders can offer a service equivalent to that of the conference, the price discount required need only be moderate, of the order say of 10 per cent. Up to about half of this may be saved by avoiding the costs of conference membership, whilst the rest might easily be covered by lines entering at a time when they can exploit changes in the cost mix.

For a line which can operate as a tolerated outsider there are a number of advantages. First it appeals to the psychological need in the market place for an alternative to the conference. Second, the policy of rate cutting may allow the line to fill its ships even if load factors generally are rather low. One particular strategy which might be adopted is to cream high rated cargoes. On large routes these are spread across the lines, and by cutting rates at the upper end of the market, the outsider can fill his ships and simultaneously obtain a higher average revenue than the conference lines. This type of competition clearly leads to a narrowing of price differentials, particularly on the shorter routes. Another option available to the outsider is to set rates to obtain particular types of cargoes, so as to improve the balance of his box movements, and this approach can sometimes be used by lines operating broad networks and trying to balance movements on a network wide basis. This may be one reason why even large conference oriented lines select outsider strategies in some areas.

This discussion started with open conference routes, but what if the

conference were closed?   The right to refuse conference membership
itself would not make much difference given the fact that the outsider
strategy is often preferred.   It is only if the conference in
association with one of its consortia could offer a guarantee of
revenues and a satisfactory load factor that there would be a strong
incentive to join.   So that although much of the attention in the past
has been given to the fact that closed conferences could exclude new
lines from membership this is not now such a powerful weapon.   On most
if not all routes of the world individual lines, provided they are of
sufficient size and have adequate backing, can obtain the scale
necessary to operate effectively as outsiders.   Thus the main question
for closed conferences is whether they could attract all important
competitors into the fold whilst at the same time keeping capacity in
line with demand.

The conferences can either tolerate outsider attack, allowing freedom to
operate under their rate umbrella, or they can fight it with a rate war.
The smaller the outsider share of total traffic and the more selective
the attack with respect to its impact on individual lines, the more
likely is the conference to vote for tolerance.   The fact that voting
rights are based simply on membership of the conference rather than on
the amount of cargo carried may often increase this inertia.   Although
conference responses have become more flexible in recent years, they
are still not flexible enough for some lines which have asked for
freedom of independent rate action.   This would give the conference as
a whole the power of selectivity in its response, and has been attacked
by outsiders as the equivalent of the use of fighting ships, a practice
usually considered to be predatory and prohibited by law in many
countries.

Once service oriented outsiders become established on a route the
competitive position changes.   First the minimum scale of outsider
entry is reduced as the outsider option begins to achieve a breadth and
credibility with shippers which may rival that of the conference itself.
Second, as outsider penetration of the route increases there is an
increasing tendency for the conference to respond, or if it is unwilling
to do so, for some lines to leave and start a rate war on their own.
Even though conference membership may later be re-established this
competitive process will tend in the long run to weaken the basis of
conference power.

Although outsiders provide a great deal of the competition on large
routes pressures can also arise within conferences.   This is partly the
result of new lines coming into established routes as conference members
and demanding shares appropriate to cargo generation in their countries
of origin.   The breadth of modern container transport networks also
allows most of the lines to trade broadly within the conference
hinterland, whereas in the conventional era there was some degree of
regional specialisation.   The failure of cargo to grow as anticipated,
or exchange rate variation which reduces cargo flows on one leg of a
route can also create pressures within the conference.   One example of
this was that of Seatrain on the North Atlantic.   It was the need to
seek higher revenues on a leg weakened by exchange rate variation which
forced the line to leave the westbound conference from the Continent and
precipitate a rate war which was the final factor leading to its own
demise.

To bring this argument back to the models discussed in Chapter 6 it may be focussed on the question of market entry. Traditional models suggest that the closed conference system provides an effective deterrent to entry to the market, whilst the open conference positively encourages it. Here it is argued that the two distinguishing features of the closed conference system, its membership conditions and strong tying arrangements, although important, do not by themselves constitute a sufficient barrier to entry. Where they do work effectively it is because the nature of the route is such that it offers only unattractive opportunities to new entrants in terms of the combination of size of investment required, relative efficiency of the proposed service and prospects of retaliation. These in turn depend very much on those aspects of route character and competitive strategy discussed above. Similarly, neither the open nature of membership nor super normal profits provide an explanation of over capacity on open conference routes, which also depends upon the characteristics of individual markets and pressures in the world at large. In reality both systems may suffer from over capacity on the type of route that attracts competition, and both respond with rate cutting, the severity of rate wars depending upon the extent of over supply, the strength of the contestants and the barriers to exit.

One point which is debatable is the importance of closed membership on those routes where strong tying arrangements are supported by the characteristics of the route. Here it could be argued conditions support the COAR system and the closed conference then becomes the basis for rationalisation. This may be true, but it could be that even if such a conference were open it would not help new entrants too much unless they were also allowed to join the operating consortium. The new entrant would still have the problem that operation at full scale would reduce load factors dramatically which could easily lead to the break up of the conference and price warfare: whilst if he operated only the occasional ship, although there would be no penalty for shippers using it, there would also be no particular advantage. Finally, the operation of an infrequent service would be likely to carry high penalties in terms of operating costs, and particularly in the cost of containers.

8 Market profiles

Introduction

In this comparative study of the experience of open and closed conferences it is clearly necessary to include the two large open conference routes, the Atlantic and the Pacific, as well as the large closed conference route from North West Europe to the Far East. Together these three account for about one half the capacity shown in Table 3.1. In addition the smaller closed conference routes from North West Europe to Australasia and South Africa will be included. These have been cited as good examples of the COAR system and proof of its effectiveness, and it is important to see how much of their success may be attributed to the character of the route in question and how much to closed conference organisation. Any comparison of conference activity faces the problem that change is continuous and often at a hectic pace, whilst it is only possible to follow events, for a limited period - in this case from 1980 to the Summer of 1982. Nevertheless the period has been one in which both systems have been responding to tremendous pressures, and provides a fair indication of their operation.

The analysis starts with a set of tables showing a breakdown of capacity by shipping line in 1980 for major geographical areas, each of which covers a number of conferences. The tables were produced in the Marine Transport Centre by a cumulation of voyages as recorded in Lloyds Voyage Records. Interpretation of the tables and of developments over the last two years has been greatly helped by discussion with shipping lines and conference secretariats, as well as by reports in the trade press, particularly Containerisation International.

EUROPE TO AUSTRALASIA

The route from North West Europe to Australasia has a distance of some 26,000 n.m., although this can be shortened somewhat for those ships which return from New Zealand via Panama. Many of the features of the COAR system were developed on this route and by the time it was containerised in 1970 there was an established tradition of co-operation and rationalisation. This was a great help to the consortia which containerised the continental/UK sector of the route, as pooling arrangements were in place which allowed a reduction in fleet size from over sixty conventional liners to nine 23 knot cellular containerships of 1,500 TEUs. A second service operates from Scandinavia. This carries a large volume of non containerised semi-bulk cargoes as well as containers, and uses ro-ro container ships.

The early attempt to operate 63 day round trips was abandoned, partly because of increasing fuel costs and the need to slow down and partly because of poor port performance in both Australia and New Zealand. In an analysis based on the 1977 Voyage Records it was shown that round trips were of eleven and twelve weeks duration, with about 30 per cent of the total spent in port. On the shorter Far East route using rather larger ships the TRIO service spends only about 25 per cent of time in port, whilst with slightly smaller ships the ACE service spends only 20 per cent. (Pearson 1980). It is a somewhat curious phenomenon that with all the attention given to conference freight rates and efficiency of operation, a level of port performance at one end of the route which requires an additional two ships in the fleet, as well as severely impairing service quality, has been tolerated by government, shippers and marketing boards alike since containers were introduced.

Table 8.1 shows the position on the route in 1980. At first sight ship size looks a bit low for such a long route, but there are in fact some very large cellular ships employed, the rated capacity of which is reduced by a high proportion of refrigerated space. The route receives a weekly cellular container service and a fortnightly ro-ro service both operated by conference lines, and in 1980 these provided some 90 per cent of throughput. It is relatively isolated geographically and the only alternatives to direct services are by combinations of the Trans Siberian Railway and the Japan Australasian routes, or the Europe US West Coast route and the Pacific. These have been tried by non vessel owning common carriers (NVOCCs) but have not had a great deal of impact. Non conference services are provided by Polish Ocean Lines and ABC, and although the capacities shown for 1980 are rather small ABC was in the process of mounting an important competitive assault on the route.

The ABC service began with a contract signed in 1978 with E.I. Du Pont De Nemours to carry 300,000 tonnes per annum of mineral sands from Geraldton in Western Australia to Gulf Port Mississippi. This was used as the basis for a round the world bulk container service with ships which have been described in some detail in Chapter 3. The ships were built in the Cockerill yard Belgium and ABC as a Belgian line obtained them on very favourable terms. For example two 1,720 TEU ships with 740 TEUs of expensive refrigerated capacity cost only US $32 million each. Of this only 15 per cent was required as a down payment the rest being repayable over 17 years at a rate of interest of $1\frac{1}{2}$ per cent.

Services began in September 1978 and built up to a three weekly frequency in 1980 operated with six bulk container ships. There is a very long itinerary with UK, Benelux, German and Mediterranean calls as well as five Australian calls, one in New Zealand, two in the US Gulf and one in Philadelphia for the meat contract on the US Australia route. There is a feeder service to Scandinavia and plans to add occasional direct calls to Gothenburg, whilst alternate sailings out of Europe are routed via South Africa. Given a relatively slow ship speed, extended itinerary, long service interval, and variation in ship capacity, service quality is well below that of the conference. However, on the basis of competitive prices the service has been able to survive and even grow. Two ships were added to the fleet in 1982 to improve frequency to

Table 8.1

Europe to Australasia - 1980

	Capacity 000 TEUs	One Way Trips	Average Ship Size TEUs
Conference			
ACT (A)	43	28	1,529
ANL	26	16	1,602
CGM	30	18	1,307
Hapag Lloyd	22	13	1,660
NedLloyd	23	12	1,931
OCL	93	54	1,715
Scan Carriers	64	40	1,593
Other	32	24	1,356
Total Conference	333	205	1,624
Outsiders			
ABC	15	15	1,018
Columbus	2	2	950
Polish Ocean	12	30	393
Others	9	25	364
Total Outsiders	38	72	527
Route Total	370	280	1,312

fourteen days, and there was talk, some of it rather exaggerated, of building up to an eventual total of sixteen.

One aspect of the Europe Australia route is the low Australian participation. Shortly after starting operations ABC sold a one third share in the line to three Australian companies, Thomas Nationwide Transport, Bell Freight Lines and the Smorgon Group, and this was later raised to 50 per cent. This gave it at least a partial Australian identity, as well as a domestic transport capability and a link with meat export interests.

The ABC approach shows how even such apparently unpromising territory as the Europe Australia route can be subjected to competition. First the line uses flexible ships and operates on a scale which requires only a small share of the container market. Second the deal with Cockerill Yards provided finance at a rate of interest so far below the rate of inflation that the line obtained its ships at exceptionally favourable rates. Third there is alignment with national interests, exploiting an imbalance between Australian cargo generation and flag shares and fourth, a degree of integration with shippers and local transport interests in Australia. In 1981 ABC joined the Australia US conference for its meat export contract but basically requires to operate with a price differential to counter a relatively low service quality, and this move proved to be short lived. Although it would doubtless like the position of tolerated outsider the line is quite rightly perceived as a major threat to the conference and has been responsible for a substantial cut in freight rates.

In the Australian trades generally it is possible to discern a quite deliberate policy on the part of the Marketing Boards to bring outsiders into the trade and use them as levers in rate negotiations with the conference lines. On some routes they have been given a substantial share of major export cargoes and even where this is not done they may be given 'experimental' shipments to maintain interest. The policy seems to have been quite successful from the exporters point of view as there has been some rate cutting, and in contract negotiations with the conference rate increases have been rather below the rate of inflation. It could well be that the long term policy is to sustain the conference and simply to ensure that there is some genuine competitive action on the route. Whatever the policy it is a far cry from the cosy COAR system in which rate discussions are based on an independently verified calculation of costs within the conference, without reference to outside competition.

EUROPE SOUTH AFRICA

The Europe South Africa route was containerised as recently as 1977. With a round trip length of about 13,000 n.m., it is approximately half the length of the Australasian route and has slightly less traffic. But it is a less dispersed route with a high standard of port performance and large ships are employed. The main service is supported with a feeder operated by Unicorn Lines, which prevents the itinerary becoming too extended, whilst at the European end there is a separate low frequency service to the Mediterranean. The route is a relatively isolated one, in that with the Suez Canal open, not many major container

Table 8.2

NW Europe - South Africa - 1980

	Capacity 000 TEUs	One Way Trips	Average Ship Size TEUs
Conference			
CMB	35	14	2,470
Deutsche Afrika Linien	40	18	2,238
Ellerman Harrison	37	15	2,450
Safmarine	140	58	2,413
CGM	7	10	680
Total Conference	259	115	2,252
Outsiders	8	15	549

Mediterranean - South Africa - 1980

	Capacity 000 TEUs	One Way Trips	Average Ship Size TEUs
Conference			
Lloyd Triestino	31	24	1,309
Safmarine	17	13	1,309

services come near it and there is no threat from overland routes or trans-shipment. The lines concentrated on large cellular ships with slow speed diesels and a speed of 23 knots, but they did not anticipate the decline of traffic which was to take place in the late 1970s and the route was to some extent over provided. This has, however, been met by chartering some of the tonnage and also by a programme of selective slow steaming.

A feature of the route illustrated in Table 8.2 is the division among trading partners. Three European lines representing Belgium, Germany and the UK combine to provide 50 per cent of the capacity on the major North West European sector, whilst the rest is provided by the South African Line in which the government has a substantial interest. On the smaller Mediterranean sector Safmarine combines with Lloyd Triestino, although in this case the Italian line had the major share, at least in 1980.

This route is undoubtedly the most stable of those examined in this chapter and was the least subject to outsider competition in 1980, but it is clearly one where the forces of competition are naturally rather subdued.

EUROPE TO THE FAR EAST

Europe to the Far East is the largest of the closed conference routes with a capacity of some 1,300,000 TEUs in shipping services in 1980, to which must be added a further 100,000 or so from the Trans Siberian Railway. It is a long route of some 22,400 n.m., via Suez and at speeds now usually sailed requires a nine week round trip. It is also a rather complicated route with a large number of trading nations at both ends and some degree of specialisation in itineraries. In the Far East the route serves Japan, the most dynamic trading nation in the post war world, together with a number of newly industrialising nations including Korea, Taiwan, Singapore, Malaysia and Hong Kong, most of which have also sustained high levels of economic growth. It also handles Chinese traffic although China is now developing its own maritime capability and domestic container ports.

As well as land bridge competition from the Trans Siberian Railway there is competition to North Continent services from the Mediterranean sector. Of the total capacity provided by water in 1980 some 190,000 TEUs was in services which terminated in Mediterranean ports, whilst some of the North Continent services also included a Mediterranean call. The route was containerised in the early 1970s with third generation cellular containerships of up to 3,000 TEUs, many of which were equipped with steam turbine engines and operated at speeds of 26 knots. During the later 1970s many of these ships were slow steaming and in 1979 a programme of re-engining with slow speed diesels was embarked upon by many lines, service speeds being reduced to about 21 knots.

Tables 8.3 and 8.4 show capacities and market shares on the Continental and Mediterranean sectors. The important Continental sector is dominated by three large consortia, TRIO, SCAN DUTCH and ACE, which together provided almost one million TEUs capacity in 1980. The largest of these is the TRIO group, a consortium of established UK,

German and Japanese lines, which operated two services a week with eighteen third generation ships. The SCAN DUTCH group is predominantly European, with French, Dutch and Scandinavian participation as well as a new Malaysian line and ran one weekly service also with third generation ships. Finally, the ACE consortium has some European participation but is dominated by Far Eastern interests with one Japanese, two Korean, one Singapore and one Hong Kong line. ACE also provided a weekly service in 1980 but with rather smaller ships. In addition to this there is one large independent conference member, the Danish Maersk Line. Outsider participation in the route was provided by Evergreen, a large Taiwanese line, a group of COMECON lines and a number of other rather small scale operators. In 1980 outsiders plus the Trans Siberian Railway provided just over a quarter of total capacity on the route.

Throughout the early and mid 1970s the Far East Freight Conference (FEFC) and its member consortia maintained a considerable degree of control although facing quite severe competition both from the Trans Siberian Railway and Evergreen. In the later 1970s this pressure seemed to moderate somewhat, but there was a build up of capacity within the conference as the newly industrialising countries of the Far East established containerlines and used their political muscle to enter the conference and claim a share of the traffic. Thus there was a substantial growth in the capacity offered by OOCL, NOL, KSC and Cho Yang within the ACE group and by MISC within SCAN DUTCH. The established European and Japanese lines held back, but in a weakening market this could not prevent the development of over capacity. During 1981 load factors fell and rebating, which had always been a feature of this route, became more widespread with discounts ranging from 20 per cent to an extraordinary 50 per cent in some cases. Finally in November 1971 the Danish line Maersk, which with its small territorial base has been unable to negotiate an acceptable share and loading rights, (and was also dissatisfied with inadequate policing of freight rates and the very slow progress towards commodity box rates) announced its intention to leave the conference by June 1982.

Although Maersk has only a small share of the trade it is a powerful line well able to sustain an independent challenge. Its four ships operate at rather high speeds to provide a fortnightly service, and it combines fast transit times with an enviable reputation for reliability. The line immediately set about making plans for a feeder service to the UK and established a marketing set up. At the same time it planned to pre-empt the conference by setting up its own simplified system of commodity box rates. With the prospect of outsider competition from Maersk as well as Evergreen, other smaller lines and the Trans Siberian Railway it looked as if the whole structure of the conference was under threat. However, in a series of moves and negotiations in the second quarter of 1982 the situation was apparently retrieved.

First in an attempt to re-establish price control the conference introduced a set of Temporarily Reduced Rates (TRR) averaging some 20 per cent below the previous level. At the same time revised internal policing arrangements were devised to be introduced in stages during the second half of 1982, and the FEFC hoped that the combination of this with TRR would reduce rebating to less than 10 per cent of its previous extent by the end of the year. Commodity box rates were also

Table 8.3

North West Europe to the Far East - 1980

	North West Europe			North West Europe and Mediterranean		
	Capacity 000 TEUs	One Way Trips	Average Ship Size TEUs	Capacity 000 TEUs	One Way Trips	Average Ship Size TEUs
Conference						
TRIO						
Ben Line	97	36	2,670			
Hapag Lloyd	137	48	2,858	6	4	1,582
Mitsui Osk	53	27	1,950			
NYK Line	81	37	2,177			
OCL	149	59	2,522			
	516	207	2,493	6	4	1,582
SCAN DUTCH						
CGM	10	6	1,726	25	9	2,800
MISC	5	2	2,450	47	19	2,450
Nedlloyd	-	-	-	87	30	2,913
Brostroms	5	2	2,441	84	34	2,464
	20	10	2,014	243	92	2,641
ACE						
CMB & CR	45	31	1,466			
K Line	37	16	2,298			
KSC	30	20	1,500			
NOL	36	22	1,624			
OOCL	52	30	1,749			
Cho Yang	Entered late 1980					
	200	119	1,684			
Other						
Maersk Line	35	32	1,095			
Total Conference	771	368		249	96	
Outsiders						
Evergreen	102	70	1,457			
Comecon	41	64	642	4	10	415
Others	33	48	680	13	18	698
Total Outsiders	176	182		17	28	
Route Total	948	550		266	124	

68

Table 8.4

Mediterranean to the Far East - 1980

	Capacity OOO TEUs	One Way Trips	Average Ship Size TEUs
Conference			
Mitsui Osk	14	10	1,406
NYK	14	10	1,409
Lloyd Triestino	30	22	1,382
C.R.	17	12	1,402
Lauro Line	7	5	1,454
Total Conference	83	59	1,401
Outsiders			
Evergreen	36	53	689
Comecon & Others	71	106	670
Total Outsiders	107	159	672

introduced for a number of important items in the eastbound trade. These moves helped provide the basis for an agreement with Maersk. In negotiations just prior to its impending withdrawal from the conference the line was offered an increased share of traffic, together with loading rights in the UK and Eire, and on this basis it signed a further three year agreement with the conference. In a separate though related move the conference reached an accommodation with Evergreen. There was an agreement on capacity with release by Evergreen of some of its market share, although the extent of this in a market in which cargo was declining anyway, is arguable. In return for this the line was given a form of tolerated outsider status. Shippers in the Far East excluding Japan will be allowed to ship with Evergreen without loss of their deferred rebate on conference cargo, whilst at the same time the Evergreen discount from the conference tariff will be held to not more than 5 per cent. (The exclusion of Japanese shippers stems from the special nature of their contractual relationship with the conference). For Evergreen, which depends in its westbound trade on certain special contracts with large shippers, this was probably as far as it was possible to go in reaching agreement with the conference.

The FEFC encountered some criticism from shippers in relation to these moves. The European Shippers' Council criticised the timing and speed of introduction of commodity box rates, whilst both they and the British Shippers' Council criticised the idea of Temporarily Reduced Rates, arguing that any reduction in rates should be considered to be part of the conference tariff, not to be increased without the normal processes of consultation. Finally the Japanese Shippers' Council took issue with the Evergreen deal, arguing that their members should receive similar treatment to other shippers in the Far East.

However, it does seem as if the FEFC is in the process of re-establishing control of rates and shares; and the need of both conference lines and outsiders for stability must clearly have been very strong for these complex negotiations to be successfully concluded in a weak market.

THE ATLANTIC ROUTES

The Atlantic routes are the second largest group in the world comprising a very large sector to the US East Coast together with smaller routes to Canada, the US Gulf and West Coast. The US East Coast and Canadian routes are strongly linked, with some Canadian cargo finding its way through US ports and probably something of the order of 60 per cent of traffic through Canadian ports being destined for US markets, particularly those of Chicago and the Mid West. At around 7,000 n.m. for the round trip these routes are relatively short with the main options being for 21 and 28 day round trips. There is also a maximum economic ship size in the region of 1,500 TEUs.

The Gulf route is much longer with a round trip of some 11,000 n.m., but it has a very much lower traffic density. There is also competition between the Gulf route and the US East Coast which is extending its influence to the South. Finally there is the very long route to the West Coast which had only some 241,000 TEUs capacity in 1980. This also receives mini bridge competition from the Gulf route and to some extent from the East Coast route.

All trades through US ports are under the jurisdiction of the FMC and operate under an open conference system. Canadian services are however, outside FMC jurisdiction.

The US East Coast and Canada

Table 8.5 shows the Canadian and East Coast routes at a time of intense competition. There have been many changes since then, but 1980 is a good starting point for discussion of the route and consideration of open conference functioning.

At the beginning of 1980 there were seven main conference lines (including Seatrain) on the US East Coast which together held about 80 per cent of total capacity. But if we take the two routes together and include the Canadian gateway the conferences had only a 72 per cent share. The two major outsiders were Trans Freight Lines, which entered the US market in 1978 in a period of relatively prosperous conditions and low outsider participation, and CAST who operate bulk container ships through Montreal. Trans Freight Lines is a service oriented company which sets its prices at a small discount from the conference, this being covered by savings on conference membership plus the advantages of operating modern diesel engined ships under the Singapore flag. CAST is very different, operating on the basis of low cost and a substantial price discount for a service which is below that of the conference. Most of the other outsiders in 1980 were rather

Table 8.5

NW Europe to the US East Coast & Canada - 1980

	East Coast			St. Lawrence & Gt. Lakes		
	Capacity 000 TEUs	One Way Trips	Average Ship Size TEUs	Capacity 000 TEUs	One Way Trips	Average Ship Size TEUs
Conference						
ACL	251	281	884	33	61	540
Dart	161	101	1,590			
Hapag Lloyd	185	107	1,728			
Sea-Land	257	156	1,648			
US Lines	196	190	1,009			
Farrell	81	82	1,000			
CP Ships				68	92	755
Manchester Liners				52	101	519
Total Conference	1,131	917		153	254	
Major Outsiders						
Polish Ocean	32	93	350			
CAST				93	60	765
Seatrain	92	87	1,087			
Trans Freight Lines	125	137	912			
	250	317		93	60	
Minor Outsiders						
Falline Blasco				21	56	374
Star Shipping	12	15	799	6	5	1,200
Contract Marine	21	54	391			
Waterman	23	28	820			
Lusitainer	5	32	152			
Others	37	–	–	18	–	–
	98			45		
Route Total	1,481			291		

small, although in earlier years the Russian line Balt Atlantic had operated on a large scale.

In late 1979 Seatrain announced its resignation from the continental westbound conference, this becoming effective in February 1980. It cited as its reason for this its inability to compete effectively with outsiders. But the decision was influenced by the generally weak financial position of the line and by changes in foreign exchange rates which had reduced the flow of west bound cargo. Following a series of meetings within the conference in which the other American lines threatened to withdraw, it was finally agreed that a clause within the agreement which allowed for independent rate action in an emergency should be invoked. Rates which had been barely remunerative at the beginning of the year were slashed by between 25 and 50 per cent with the average reduction being estimated at about 30 per cent. By the end of March rate action had affected 1,300 items in 4,500 separate changes. During this period the conference acted largely as a vehicle for filing new rates with the FMC, such reductions becoming effective immediately, although increases require 90 days notice. In filing their new rates the conference lines were attempting to approach or possibly to equal those of competitors, any reduction below this being capable of interpretation as unlawfully predatory under US law. After the first few months some order was restored in the form of a weekly meeting in which lines would negotiate rates to match the competition, although the right of independent action was retained.

In July 1980 Eurobridge Lines, a small outsider, withdrew from the route and in September Seatrain went into liquidation, concluding deals with Trans Freight Lines for the purchase of its offices and goodwill and with CAST for the purchase of many of its containers. Finally, in November Farrell Lines withdrew. The pace of rate action slowed down in the latter part of 1980 and in January 1981 the conference re-established its tariff at 4 per cent above the level of December 1979. There was a further reduction in capacity when ACL re-organised the deployment of its fleet to lay up some of its G2s, which as steam turbine engined ships were the most expensive of its fleet to operate. However, outsider capacity continued to grow somewhat as Polish Ocean Lines implemented its plans to re-enter the route with four container ro-ro ships with a projected capacity of some 115,000 TEUs per annum.

During 1981 and 1982 much of the activity on the route was in the Canadian sector including of course the Canadian gateway to US markets. In the late 1970s, following a long period of slow growth and low cost operations with cheap bulk carriers slightly modified to take containers, CAST decided upon a US $400m. programme of expansion. This covered the construction of six purpose built bulk container ships of 70,000 dwt and 1,450 TEUs on the basis of which it planned to double capacity to 180,000 TEUs per annum by 1983. At the same time, after being a 20' box operator for many years it planned to diversify into the 40' box market. In preparation for these changes CAST was very active in the market in 1981 offering low box rates from origin to destination. These were not so much f.a.k rates or commodity box rates as competitive rates set at whatever level necessary to secure cargo. However, early in 1982 the line was severely affected by a weakening of bulk cargo rates, and as a result of this, together with its substantial acquisition programme and relatively low rates on container carrying, it found itself in severe financial difficulties. In a complex re-structuring operation it sold three of its bulk carriers and entered into a sale and lease back arrangement for three of the new bulk container ships, and this formed part of a US $200m. package which allowed the line to continue in operation. At the same time under pressure from its creditors CAST was forced to increase its rates and had to apply a US $275 per TEU recessionary surcharge in April of 1982. Following this CAST lost much of its rate advantage and a curious situation developed in which some of its rates were for a time higher than those of the conference lines. Because of this together with uncertainties regarding its future, it lost many of its shippers.

CAST's problems coincided with a re-organisation of the Canadian services in which CP Ships, Manchester Liners and Dart formed a new consortium. A number of small ships were taken off the route, the Dart service to Halifax was discontinued, and three large ships of over 1,500 TEUs were introduced to provide a low cost weekly service and give a moderate boost to capacity. The Summer of 1982 saw CAST a traditionally aggressive line (often considered to be irresponsible in the ferocity of its rate cutting), engaged in serious negotiations with the Canadian conferences, and in mid August it announced its intention to join. At the same time the conferences planned to introduce commodity box rates to accommodate CAST's pricing strategy, and to increase rates generally to recover profitability in operations. There was also discussion of a programme for rationalising capacity. This would have involved a complicated set of arrangements by which CAST would slot charter capacity to the new co-ordinated service, which in turn would make capacity available to ACL, some of the latter consortia's small ships being taken off the route. CAST were also to be allowed to break a conference ruling which prevented the use of feeder ships in serving the UK market. Clearly a very serious attempt was being made to restore stability, but these plans were upset when in September 1982 there was a defection of CAST's senior executives. They left to start a new service, to be known as Sofati, which would operate as an outsider with three small ships of some 500 TEUs running between Tilbury, Antwerp and Montreal. This upset the whole deal and at the end of September CAST announced that it would not be joining the conference after all. ACL did, however, go ahead with its plan to withdraw its small ships from the Montreal service, re-instituting a Halifax call on its US east coast service to meet the needs of its Canadian shippers.

Looking further ahead there are no very strong signs of rationalisation in the Atlantic trades as a whole. The market is very weak and the complex inter-relationship with the Canadian gateway tends to maintain a fluid competitive situation. In the US itself, although there have been some moves towards rationalisation, there are prospects for further increases in capacity from a number of sources. These include a new American outsider who obtained the military contract for six months late in 1982, as well as ACL who are now building five 2,300 TEU container ro-ro ships with which they will run a weekly service. United States lines also have plans for a very large fleet expansion with the construction of a fleet of 14 container ships rated at over 4,000 TEUs. Although these ships would be too large for a standard North Atlantic itinerary, they might provide capacity on the Atlantic as part of a new round the world service, whilst re-organisation of the rest of US Lines fleet would also provide scope for increasing capacity in this market.

The US Gulf and West Coast Routes

Details of the US Gulf and West Coast routes are shown in Table 8.6.
The West Coast route has a very simple structure, with two conference
lines, Johnson Scanstar and Euro Pacific, providing some 150,000 TEUs
of capacity in 1980 and with Hoegh and Star Line providing a notional
86,000 TEUs in timber container carriers.   Hoegh Line competed strongly
on price with the pure container operators and were responsible for a
severe cut in rates.

The Gulf route served by four conference lines in 1980 with Sea-Land and
Hapag Lloyd predominating.   There was also a group of outsiders
including Trans Freight Lines and Bank Line as well as ABC and Star
Shipping.   As mentioned above Seatrain withdrew from the route in 1980
and Trans Freight Lines has also reduced its interest in the Gulf.

Table 8.6

NW Europe – US Gulf & West Coast

	N.W. Europe – Gulf US			N.W. Europe – West Coast North America		
	Capacity 000 TEUs	Trips	Average Ship Size TEUs	Capacity 000 TEUs	Trips	Average Ship Size TEUs
Conference						
Hapag Lloyd	87	91	951			
Johnson Scanstar				98	103	954
Seatrain	34	37	907			
Sea-Land	132	95	1,387			
Atlantic Cargo Services	31	41	754			
Euro Pacific				53	43	1,238
Total Conference	283	264	1,070	151	146	1,038
Outsiders						
Hoegh Lines				48	34	1,400
Star Shipping	10	24	403	38	36	1,059
TFL	17	19	879			
ABC	16	16	976			
Bank	25	46	542			
Others	24	59	414	4	6	595
Total Outsiders	91	164	554	90	76	1,184
Route Total	374	428		241	222	

THE PACIFIC

The container trade from North America to the Far East is the largest in
the world with almost three million TEUs capacity in 1980. At the US
end a high proportion of the cargo is generated in the East of the
country and this can move either on a sea route from East coast ports
via Panama, or via a minibridge through the Pacific coast. The
economic case for this improves quickly as cargo location moves inland
towards the mid-west as this simultaneously reduces the inland haul to
Pacific coast ports and increases that to the East coast. The Pacific
coast itself has a very long port range and this leads to a degree of
specialisation of itineraries, some calling at Los Angeles and San
Francisco, some at Seattle and Vancouver and others covering the whole
range. In the Far East, Japan is the closest country to the US, and
as the largest trading partner receives a number of dedicated services.
It is, however, close to Korea and there are also a number of Japan
Korea services and a joint conference. An extension of about 1,300n.m.
to the south is required to bring Taiwan and Hong Kong within range and
further extensions of similar length encompass Singapore, Malaysia and
the Philippines. The number of direct services reduces substantially
as the route extends, but the outer areas can also be served by feeders,
and this is a sensible approach for many lines given the cargo distribution pattern. Details of capacities and market shares are shown in
Tables 8.7 and 8.8.

As a result of strong market conditions in the mid 1970s and the
ambitions of many of the newly developing lines of the Far East capacity
began to increase rapidly towards the end of the decade. In the fully
cellular sector it rose from 1,840,000 TEUs in 1978 to 2,168,000 in
1979 and 2,486,000 in 1980. This was an increase of some 35 per cent
which was matched by growth in the smaller sectors served by ro-ro and
semi container ships. But from about 1978 onwards the US dollar began
to decline against the yen, and although this strengthened the flow of
US exports, these are relatively low value goods and the more remunerative eastbound trade went into decline. In fact cargo flows were
estimated to have dropped by about 7 per cent in 1979 at a time when
capacities were increasing by 17 per cent.

The conference had been becoming progressively weaker throughout the
1970s as many lines which were traditionally conference oriented began
to choose outsider strategies. These included some of the new Far East
lines but also companies like Hapag Lloyd, who as cross traders in a
competitive environment adopted a rather uncharacteristic market
strategy. The conferences had, however, just about held together with
support from the traditional Japanese lines, the two large American
carriers Sea-Land and APL and a number of smaller lines. The inevitable rate crisis developed in March 1980 when Sea-Land pulled out of a
dozen eastbound conferences and rate agreements. In the eleven months
to May 1980 there were twenty seven rounds of rate cutting with an
estimated total decline of about 20 per cent in the Japan Korea
conference and of 25 per cent in the Taiwan Hong Kong conference. As
a result of this, of some twenty major lines surveyed in 1981 none
reported a profit. (Containerisation International, April 1981).

Following these developments many eastbound trades were for a time
virtually dominated by outsiders. This is rather difficult to follow

75

precisely because of the large number of conferences and rate agreements, the varied choices of the lines with respect to each of them and changes in policy which occurred from time to time. A general indication is, however, given in Table 8.7 where lines are grouped on the basis of their general preferences in eastbound trades in recent years. The broad picture is that outsiders had built up a share of about 30 per cent prior to March 1980. The rate crisis and the departure of lines from the conference camp changed the balance so that in the general eastbound trades to Japan and the Far East, outsiders held about two thirds of the total traffic, whilst in the specialised west coast trade to Japan they held about one third of the total. Taking the two routes together they had over half the total capacity in the latter part of 1980.

Table 8.7

The Trans Pacific Routes - 1980

West Coast - Far East, Japan

	Capacity 000 TEUs	One Way Trips	Average Ship Size TEUs
Conference			
Japanese joint pact	79	76	1,042
APL	312	230	1,356
EAC	30	45	663
Korean Marine Transport	25	24	1,034
Lykes	41	60	707
OOCL	27	33	809
Total Conference	514	468	1,098
Outsiders			
Sea-Land	335	185	1,808
Seatrain	83	74	1,119
Hapag Lloyd	95	94	1,010
Neptune Orient	121	87	1,394
Evergreen	52	59	878
Hanjin	88	68	1,294
Yang Ming	20	25	788
Star Shipping	14	18	795
Hoegh	32	23	1,400
Comecon	43	74	582
Others	71	118	604
Total Outsiders	954	825	1,156
Route Total	1,468	1,293	

Table 8.7 (continued)

The Trans Pacific Routes – 1980

West Coast – Japan only

	Capacity 000 TEUs	One Way Trips	Average Ship Size TEUs
Conference			
Japanese joint pact	386	351	1,100
APL	37	25	1,484
Others	22	50	437
Total Conference	445	426	1,045
Outsiders			
Seatrain	100	97	1,041
Star Shipping	51	48	1,064
Seaboard Pacific	31	28	1,090
Comecon	23	32	719
Yang Ming	13	17	787
Sea-Land	3	2	1,700
Others	10	31	319
Total Outsiders	232	255	911
Route Total	677	681	

Table 8.8 shows the final sector of the route with services to the
East coast of the US, some of which also call at Pacific coast ports.
This sector is rather smaller with a total of some 755,000 TEUs
capacity in 1980.   Conference lines predominate although even here
there is a substantial presence from Zim, Evergreen, Korean Shipping
Corporation and Yang Ming, which together held almost 30 per cent of
the total capacity.

The breakdown of the conferences and rate agreements was unwelcome to
many of the lines, even the traditional outsiders like Evergreen.
However, attempts to re-constitute them were stalled for a long time by
difficulties in reducing capacity on the route (as most of the lines
had a firm long term commitment) and also by the desire of Sea-Land for
a change in conference organisation which would give it greater ability
to deal with outsiders.

Eventually some amelioration was obtained of the problem of over
capacity.   In 1981 with the demise of Seatrain the Pacific interests
of the line were taken over by C.Y. Tung who formed the OOCL Seapac
service.   Later in the year this line joined with KSC and NOL in
filing an application to run two weekly services to the East and West
coasts of the US with eighteen ships.   In this they made the somewhat

Table 8.8

US East & West Coast to the Far East - 1980

	Capacity 000 TEUs	One Way Trips	Average Ship Size TEUs
Conference			
Japanese Lines	148	81	1,824
Maersk	137	98	1,400
OOCL	90	58	1,544
US Lines	124	91	1,363
BBS	43	24	1,800
Total Conference	542	352	1,539
Outsiders			
Evergreen	26	23	1,126
KSC	38	25	1,540
Yang Ming	48	31	1,532
Zim	89	54	1,648
Others	13	12	1,057
Total Outsiders	214	145	1,473
Route Total	756	497	

exaggerated claim that capacity would be held to less than 100,000 TEUs per annum compared to over 225,000 TEUs if each were to develop separately. Nevertheless the FMC agreed that the reduction in competitive activity on the route would be justified by the benefits of reduced capacity. It considered making approval contingent upon membership by the lines of the appropriate conferences, but dropped this provision. Approval was granted in the Spring of 1982 and the two services were inaugurated in May, bringing an immediate reduction in capacity, claimed by OOCL to be of the order of 15 per cent. Perhaps more important than this was the fact that FMC approval was contingent on a limit upon the number of ships on the two routes, and this brought with it a measure of capacity control and stability.

Many of the Japanese services also operate under space charter arrange-ments filed with the FMC. These expire periodically and upon appli-cation for renewal of certain of these arrangements in 1981 the FMC began to impose capacity limits. In fact following objections from US carriers, approval procedures have become bogged down in court action. At the time of writing the outcome is uncertain but it is clear that there may be elements of capacity control on US open conference routes as soon as carriers become involved in any form of joint action.

The problems relating to the structure of competition on the route was
of a rather different character. Japanese and Far Eastern lines have
a strong hold on relatively high rated eastbound cargo originating in
their hinterlands and could probably flourish in a mixed environment
comprised of conference lines and outsiders. Sea-Land felt itself to
be vulnerable to such competition particularly if it had to abide by
conference decisions reached on the basis of one line one vote, in
conferences where other members were in a more protected position.
The solution to this was a change in conference rules in which the FMC
agreed that a group of lines within a conference would be allowed
minority rate initiative 'RI' when conference carryings of a commodity
fell below 70 per cent of the total. In July 1982 Sea-Land returned
to the important Trans Pacific Conference of Japan and Korea 'TPCJK'.
They were followed by OOCL and then surprisingly Evergreen announced
its intention to join the TPCJK in the Autumn of 1982 and the US East
Coast Conference in early 1983. This brought broad conference control
back to major sectors of the Pacific, together with a programme of rate
retrieval in which the initial intention was to regain the levels of
1979.

COMMENTARY

This review of the recent history of some major container markets
clearly indicates a mode of operation which is at variance with the
formal models of closed and open conference operation described in
Chapter 6. A major point is that conferences, even the open ones, do
not maintain rates in the face of over capacity, and rate cutting has
been fierce and sustained on a number of major routes in the last few
years. Indeed it is difficult to see any evidence of ratchet effects
at work. A second broad conclusion is that over capacity is not simply
a feature of open conference routes brought about by a failure of this
particular form of market organisation. It has been a more general
phenomenon brought about by a combination of long term trends together
with a number of special circumstances, which converged in 1980 to
produce a widespread crisis within the deep sea container shipping
industry and its conference systems. Among the main influences at work
have been the weakening of demand as major routes approach the top of
the 'S' curve of container penetration. This has been compounded by
the general weakness in international trade in recent years and by
exchange rate fluctuations which have altered cargo balance of some
major routes. At the same time there has been continued growth of
capacity. This has also been brought about by a combination of factors.
One of the most important has been the growth of new container lines
determined to obtain a place in world markets and often operating with
the support of governments or large parent companies which will support
a sustained effort. Many of these are the lines of the newly industrialising nations of the Far East and have affected chiefly the North
West Europe Far East route and the Pacific. Another important feature
has been the desire of governments to support their domestic shipbuilding
industries in a weak world market and corresponding provision of cheap
and easy finance for the purchase of new ships. In fact if one wished
to identify a single major source of the problems of the industry to
replace the old scapegoat of the open conference system, it would be
the widespread provision of support for shipping lines and the purchase
of new tonnage based on non commercial criteria. The other side of

this coin is that closed conferences are not a panacea for the industry's ills or the problems of over capacity, and the market power of the COAR system on some of the smaller routes, or indeed on the Far East route in the early and mid 1970s, owed as much to favourable circumstances as it did to the strengths of the system itself.

Turning to some of the more detailed differences between routes it seems that the general parameters identified in Chapter 7 can explain a great deal of the differences between routes and be used to rate general competitive characteristics. Thus the two small closed conference routes are shown to be significantly less competitive than the three large routes, partly because their size will not sustain more than one or two services, but also because of relative geographical isolation and, in the case of South Africa, a stable market share pattern and government involvement in Safmarine. The three large routes are all much more competitive. The Far East route has a closed conference system and in terms of its size and geographical coverage the FEFC is a very powerful body. But it has been subject to land bridge competition and outsider attack as well as strong pressures within the conference from new container lines. As a result of this it has been unable to maintain the control of rates and rationalisation of capacity tradition- ally claimed for the closed conference. Indeed for a time in early 1982 it looked as if the whole structure of the conference was under threat. The two large open conference routes of the Pacific and the Atlantic have been the most competitive of those surveyed. They are both much larger than the Europe Far East route in terms of TEU capacity, and they are also shorter; these factors tending to increase competit- iveness. There is also inter modal competition from various mini bridge routes and alternative gateways to match the land bridge operations of the Far East route. One additional factor has been the decline of the US dollar which has been a great source of instability on both routes as it has created cargo imbalances which have been the immediate cause of rate wars. On the North Atlantic there was a period of very intensive price competition in 1980. In 1981 the conference regained control of rates, but every withdrawal from the route seems to be matched by some new competitive move and no solution to the problem of over capacity is in sight. The Pacific has been the most competitive of all routes, with a breakdown of conferences and rate agreements which lasted almost two and a half years, control being regained only in late 1982. There was an element of government intervention in the reconstitution of conferences and rate agreements. This took the form of FMC monitoring of joint service arrangements and the barrier this provides to increases in capacity. At the same time there was some form of tacit accommodat- ion between the lines, in respect of future plans which might have some similarities to the bargaining which goes on within the closed conference.

It now seems that conferences generally have regained some form of control of the major routes, and since this has taken place after such fierce and extended battles it is possible that existing participants have come to terms and there may be a period of relative stability and conference control of rates. But the flow of new capacity continues. For example, completion of the new US Lines order would add substan- tially to the world fleet, whilst Evergreen is just completing a large expansion programme and Comecon fleets also seem to be contemplating new developments, to mention just a few which come readily to mind: and much of this new capacity will inevitably be deployed on the three major

routes discussed above.   In fact if the root cause of the industry's
problems lie with the sources of over capacity rather than with the
aberrations of the conference system, there may still be some way to go
before carriers can look forward with reasonable confidence to a period
of stability.

Given the differences in character between the various routes and the
importance of the general trends mentioned above it is difficult to
draw empirical conclusions on the relative merits of each form of
conference organisation.   It would be ungenerous not to acknowledge the
successes of the closed conferences in the late 1960s and early 1970s
when they were involved in the containerisation of many major routes,
but for reasons given above this does not prove the case for them.
Looking at the late 1970s and early 1980s and taking the three large
routes, where there is sufficient similarity in character for a sensible
comparison, all that can be said is that the FEFC appears to have
channelled and to some extent controlled the growth of capacity a bit
more effectively than the large open conferences.   Certainly its
periods of rate instability have been somewhat shorter and less intense
and its rates may have remained closer to a profitable or at least a
cost recovery level.   As against this negotiations over shares have
strong political elements, so that enormous pressures build up, whilst
rebating has been almost endemic.

This commentary concludes the first part of the argument relating to the
nature of competition and the general performance of closed and open
conferences.   The complex issues relating to regulatory policy will be
dealt with in succeeding chapters.   During the course of this discussion
it will be shown that there are many other characteristics of conferences
in addition to the rules regarding membership, and that it is also
necessary to broaden the scope of investigation to examine the overall
operation of regulatory regimes.

9 Regulation in the United States – 1961 – 1982

Definitions

Before going into the issues arising from regulatory policy in the US
it is necessary to distinguish between the form of regulation which
applies in the liner shipping industry and that which most often
applies in other transport modes.   The most common form of regulation
in the transport industries is the control of capacity and prices by an
agency of government.   Capacity is controlled by the issue of licenses
and the authority either has direct rate making powers or has control
over the prices set by transport operators.   The regulation of road,
rail and air transport industries has been widespread during this
century, but in the last two decades there has been a general movement
to open up these controlled industries to freer market function.   This
has had effect in Australia, the UK and the US, culminating during the
Carter administration in the de-regulation of road, rail, inland water-
ways and some sectors of aviation.   The liner shipping industry has
never been regulated in the above sense, and although the term de-
regulation is sometimes loosely applied to it, this has no clear meaning
and the general debate on de-regulation is of no direct relevance.

Where liner shipping services are dominated by closed conferences there
are important elements of centralised control and planning, although as
shown in Chapter 8, market forces continue to operate and control is not
nearly so strict as in a government regulated industry.   In the US the
situation is different as, although conferences are allowed, and the
industry can set its own prices and determine its own capacity, it
operates under supervision.   The basis of this is the Shipping Act of
1916 as subsequently amended, which set up a regulatory authority with
the responsibility for monitoring the activities of carriers and
conferences and ensuring that they conform to certain standards.
Although it was the intention of Congress that the regulatory authority
should have primacy of jurisdiction over the industry, this has
gradually been eroded so that the anti trust laws also apply.   The
regime has become a mixed one in which there are certain elements of
regulatory control, some of general supervision and some where the anti
trust laws apply as they would in an unregulated industry.

The regulatory policy of the US is extremely important in world liner
shipping, partly because of the size of US trades, which account for
about one half of total deep sea container traffic and partly because
of the unique, harsh and contentious nature of the regime itself.   As
a result of a number of pressures including the problems of the US
merchant marine, the issues of comity which have arisen and also the

general awareness of the failings of the regulatory regime itself, there has been a movement towards regulatory reform. The early development of the US regulatory regime was dealt with in Chapter 1. This chapter takes up the story with the regulatory changes of 1961 and deals with the evolution of the regime in the subsequent two decades. Following this Chapter 10 deals with the movement for reform.

THE REGULATORY REGIME AFTER 1961

Public Law 87-346 was passed in 1961 in a major revision of the Shipping Act of 1916. It replaced the old Federal Maritime Board (with its joint responsibilities for promotion and regulation) with a new Federal Maritime Commission which was to concentrate on regulation alone. In a further strengthening of supervisory powers the 'public interest' standard was added to the existing 'detrimental to commerce' and 'unjustly discriminatory' standards of Section 15 of the Act which states the basis on which agreements between carriers may be approved. The dual rate contracts which had been disallowed in the Isbrandtsen judgement were re-instated subject to a maximum spread of rates of 15 per cent, but deferred rebates were again specifically prohibited. Under the provisions of Section 18b of the Act a new discipline was imposed in that all carriers operating through US ports were required to file their tariffs with the FMC and make them available for public inspection. Individual carriers were asked to ensure that only filed tariffs were applied, whilst conferences had the responsibility for policing agreements under threat that laxity in this respect could lead to them being dis-approved. Tariffs were thereby brought under the supervision of regulatory standards with the 'detrimental to commerce of the US' standard being re-iterated in Section 18. It was, however, the clear intention of Congress that the FMC should have primacy of jurisdiction, and the initial penalties for non compliance with the new tariff filing provisions of Section 18 were relatively modest at US $ 1,000 per day.

The newly created FMC did indeed pursue its regulatory functions with great vigour. It started a number of investigations under the 'detrimental to commerce' standard, and its attempts to subpoena information from trading partners caused immediate difficulties. But however active the FMC became the regime would have been a tolerable one if it had worked as intended by Congress, and the FMC had retained primacy of jurisdiction. There was every reason to expect that this would be so, as the amendments of 1961 were made after a long period of relative quiet in legal actions against conferences, and although dual rates had been allowed regulatory supervision under the Shipping Act had also been greatly strengthened. But the Isbrandtsen case proved to be only the first of a number of legal actions, whilst following the fierce criticism of the conference system in the Celler committee the Department of Justice kept up its attack upon what it perceived to be the anti-competitive activities of regulated open conferences. As a result there was a serious erosion of anti trust immunity and weakening of the jurisdiction of the FMC.

The erosion of the anti trust immunity was important partly because the penalties under the Sherman Clayton Acts are severe. Under these Acts parties to an illegal agreement are liable in criminal proceedings to prison sentences of up to three years and in civil proceedings to compensation assessed at three times the injury suffered: and a successful criminal proceeding is of course likely to be followed immediately by a civil action. But this is not the whole story as it was intended that the Shipping Act itself should be effectively enforced. Court actions also exposed certain ambiguities in the relationship between the Shipping Act and the anti trust laws. In the process of re-statement of the law the primacy of anti trust legislation (which has a very high status with the US legal regime) was re-affirmed in such a way that the regulatory standards of the Act took on a new meaning. As a result they came to impose severe limitations upon the freedoms with which carriers, consortia and conferences could operate and plan ahead.

The Erosion of Anti-Trust Immunity

The first important breach of the FMC's jurisdiction was in <u>Carnation v the Pacific Westbound Conference 1966</u>. Carnation as a large shipper brought a treble damages suit under the Clayton Act alleging that the conference had used an unfiled rate to discriminate against it. A district court dismissed the action on the grounds that the matter was within the jurisdiction of the FMC; but this decision was reversed by the supreme court which held that the courts had an obligation to enforce the nation's fundamental national policy and hear the suit. As a result of this, violations of the Shipping Act became a matter for the anti trust laws in spite of the fact that there were clear provisions within the Shipping Act itself to deal with them.

The second important case was that of the <u>FMC v Aktiebolaget Svenska Linien 1968</u>. In a judgement in this case the supreme court affirmed the use of an anti trust standard as a method of weighing the public interest. This is stated in the following terms :

> "The parties seeking exemption from the anti trust laws for their agreement must demonstrate that the agreement is required by a serious transportation need, or in order to secure important public benefits. Otherwise it is our view that the public interest in the preservation of competition where possible, even in regulated industries is unduly offended, and the agreement is contrary to that interest within the meaning of Section 15 .... Disapproval of an agreement on this basis is not founded in any necessary finding that it violates the anti trust laws but rather because the anti-competitive activity under agreement invades the prohibitions of the anti trust laws more than is necessary to serve the purpose of the Shipping Act and is therefore contrary to the public interest."

This judgement was of profound importance because although the intention of the Shipping Act was that the FMC should approve all agreements other than those it found to be contrary to the provisions of the Act or the regulatory standards, the Svenska decision placed the burden of proof that an agreement was not contrary to the public interest on the carriers. Further, to provide this proof they would have to show that the agreement would yield some continuing benefit over the notionally more competitive situation that would exist without it. A similar case which was decided at the same time concerned the Sabre Line whose entry into the Pacific as an outsider in the late 1960s precipitated a rate war. The line took the conference to court arguing that rates were unreasonably low (i.e. predatory) under the meaning of Section 18 of the Shipping Act. In Sabre Shipping Corporation v American President Lines Ltd. 1968 the court held that, even where rates were approved and filed, if it could be demonstrated subsequently that they were so high or low as to be detrimental to US commerce they would be in contravention of Section 18 of the Act, and therefore unlawful, exposing the lines to the anti trust laws.

In 1973 Seatrain filed a protest against the takeover by PFEL of the fleet and other maritime interests of the Oceanic Steamship Co. Although it was stripped of its assets Oceanic was free to re-enter the Pacific coast/Australia trade. The FMC refused Seatrain's request and approved the agreement. In Seatrain Lines v the FMC the supreme court reversed this arguing that as the proposed merger eliminated one of the parties to the agreement, whilst imposing no obligations on the signatories, it was outside the scope of Section 15 which was limited to ongoing agreements under continuous FMC supervision.

In 1982 a further long drawn out case against the North Atlantic lines was drawn to its conclusion. The conferences on this route faced a number of difficulties arising out of its geographical complexity and the nature of inter conference competition. European shippers complained of anomalies and there was even at one time a suggestion by the FMC that the carriers should form a super conference. An application was made to implement this which foundered under opposition including that of the Department of Justice. The Department continued its investigations into rate setting and as a result the allegation was made that between 1971 and 1979, the lines fixed rates outside the scope of approved agreements, in some cases because the agreements themselves were not approved and in others because procedures for approval had not been correctly followed. In the initial criminal case the lines pleaded 'no lo contendere' and accepted fines of some US $4 million. Following this a set of treble damage suits was brought by shippers. The case threatened to become extremely long and costly, to absorb an enormous amount of executive time and to impede the progress of measures for regulatory reform. Rather than pursue this course the lines offered a settlement of US $51 million, which was accepted by the courts in January 1982.

A Critique of Regulatory Standards

Both in 1916 and 1961 it was the intention of Congress that the Shipping Act should fulfil its function in large measure by the application of regulatory standards. Superficially these would seem to embody high ideals relating to justice, fairness and the public interest against which it is impossible to argue. But they have quite specific effects upon the operation of the industry which have clearly caused enormous difficulties. It is perfectly in order to challenge the interpretation and effects of standards to ask whether in reality they can fulfil the high ideals they embody, or indeed make any sense at all in the context of the operation of the liner shipping industry.

The standards of Section 15 of the Shipping Act are that agreements between carriers should not be :

"unjustly discriminatory or unfair as between carriers,
shippers, exporters, importers or ports, or between exporters,
of the United States and their foreign competitors or operate
to the detriment of the commerce of the United States or be
contrary to the public interest."

Section 18 states :

"That the Commission shall disapprove any rate it finds to be so
unreasonably high or low as to be detrimental to the commerce
of the United States."

As applied to shippers the unjustly discriminatory standard contains a
genuine safeguard, as it protects them from a refusal of conferences to
provide services to those they dislike - for whatever reason.   It also
reinforces the common carrier obligation to treat shippers alike and
meet the needs of the trade.   In reality the natural operation of the
market tends to lead to lower rates for the larger shippers, partly
because it is often somewhat cheaper to handle large volumes and partly
because outsiders tend to concentrate on them in bidding for custom.
Provided that volume rates (available to all shippers) are not regarded
as unjustly discriminatory this aspect of the standard would appear to
be equitable.

Conferences traditionally did not discriminate as between ports.   Indeed
one of the defining features of the system was that ocean freight rates
would be the same for all ports within a particular conference boundary
unless volumes were very low.   This is still the case but they have
begun to charge door to door rates and will sometimes miss out ports,
moving cargo overland from more distant locations and absorbing at least
part of the cost.   This process has been described in detail in Chapter
5 where the reasons for changes in transport system geography and port
hinterlands have been explored.   The changes are a natural result of
the development of inter modal transport, but there has been strong
resistance in the US where it was believed that there is some element
of natural right inherent in port hinterlands.   In the early years it
was extremely difficult for shipping lines to quote inter modal rates
with any degree of absorption of inland costs.   Given the enormous
pressures for change there has been an inevitable gradual easing in
this position and individual carriers can now file mini bridge rates.
These rights have not, however, been given to conferences and their
freedom in inter modal operations is severely restricted.   On occasion
this leads to great pressures within the conference as some of the
individual carriers come up against outsider competition of a type which
would normally be met with mini bridge rates.   Although ports as
servants of their local communities might in the past have had a case
for regulatory support, this is no longer valid.   Ports themselves
surely have no right to claim the equivalent of a monopoly of local
cargoes either as the by-product of an act to regulate the shipping
industry, or on the basis of an outdated view of natural port hinterlands.

At this point it is necessary to mention the Jones Act which controls
coastal shipping in the US and prevents foreign carriers from using
their own ships for trans-shipment.   Many nations have legislation to
reserve their coastal trade for domestic carriers, but in most cases

they allow overseas cargo which is being trans-shipped to be moved by foreign lines. US carriers have made great use of this particularly Sea-Land with its extensive feeder services and relays in Europe. The prohibition of the Jones Act is a limitation on operational freedom which could well be regarded as unjustly discriminatory, as between carriers.

From time to time there has been great concern expressed in the United States about possible discrimination in rates against domestic exporters and there have been a number of FMC investigations on this subject. These have invariably tended to confirm that where there is a difference in rates between the inbound and outbound legs of a route, this is the result of variations in the volume of cargo, with a natural tendency towards lower rates on the lighter legs. It is, therefore, the result of market forces rather than conspiracy.

There has also been a long debate on the nature of predatory practice and the use of 'unjustifiably low' rates by conferences against out-siders, and the Department of Justice has been particularly concerned with this aspect of conference activities. Although conferences have generally been allowed to compete on price, they are usually limited to setting rates at just above the level of outsider competition and even this has often been criticised as predatory, on the basis that rates may bear no very close relationship to cost. This criticism ignores the nature of competitive practice. When an outsider enters a route it almost invariably has to be on the basis of a competitive price as it is difficult to match the conference in service quality. A conference response to just above the level of the outsider rate could well prevent him from making any progress in the market. The outsider would then need to re-establish a rate differential and this process could continue until either the outsider went out of business or the conference was at some point prepared to tolerate the differential. Clearly with the high costs associated with market exit, rate wars can become severe, each move in the game being individually justified on the basis of an improvement in load factor and reduction in cost per unit of cargo carried, and each being nullified by the competitive response. During this process rates could clearly become non compensatory, but to call a particular conference rate unjustifiably low or predatory in this context becomes an arbitrary value judgement.

The feeling behind the prohibition of predatory practice or unjust-ifiably low rates is that the conference is the big bad wolf attacking small newcomers who are doing their best to earn a decent living by being efficient and offering good service. This may be so, but equally conference lines may be efficient and concerned to offer a high quality service, encourage trade and meet all common carrier requirements, whilst outsiders could be entering the market on the basis of subsidy and a limited service, which does not meet the needs of the trade as a whole and succeeds only by virtue of a parasitic relationship with the conference itself. Certainly a knowledge of outsiders does not suggest they are all knights of the market place, and in some cases they may be large and powerful lines choosing combinations of conference and out-sider strategies according to their reading of individual market situa-tions. Although it has been accepted since the turn of the century that conferences should be prevented from the use of certain types of competitive response like fighting ships, it would clearly be inequitable to prevent them from fighting back at outsider competition by cutting rates. There is also an element of contradiction in attacking conferences for their anti competitive activities, whilst at the same time tending to label competitive moves as predatory.

For all of the standards dealt with so far it is possible to discern a reasonably clear intention and definable scope even if one considers them to be uneconomic in their application or contain internal contradictions. The public interest standard is different because under the anti trust method for weighing the public interest, an application to file an agreement has to be judged against the hypothetically more competitive situation which would prevail in its absence. This is not a test of the market place itself but of scenarios developed by applicants, presented to the FMC Commissioners for their approval and, in the case of conflict, taken to the courts.

The Svenska interpretation of the public interest standard can be criticised on the basis of certain modern developments in economic theory, and particularly second best theory, which holds than in an imperfect situation, where prices do not reflect costs, the operation of the market is unlikely to lead towards an economic optimum. Similarly the whole idea of assessing the merits of one particular agreement against a competitive ideal, in a market place which is dominated by other agreements, must be of very doubtful validity. In fact the arguments made in applications to file agreements can not really live up to the strict requirements of this standard. They are necessarily pitched at a pragmatic level with cases for consortium agreements typically arguing for a reduction in capacity in an overcrowded market, or that a proposed service will fill a gap in the market. This could in principle allow the review process to work in a sensible way, provided that the Commissioners could be relied upon for fair, consistent and predictable judgement. This is difficult to be sure of, given the fact that they sometimes disagree, whilst personalities and political currents also affect decisions.

There is one other problem with the operation of the regulatory system generally, which is the modern practice of giving approval for only relatively short periods. This is intended to prevent abuse and ensure continuous conformity with regulatory standards. But the effect is to create enormous uncertainty with respect to future ability to operate in the market. A consortium in particular has to make a long term commitment to a service on the basis of short term approval, and has absolutely no guarantee of future renewal on a satisfactory basis. Further to this the application can be objected to by other interests including competing shipping lines, and approval is then almost certain to be long delayed or costly, whatever the eventual outcome. In actions of this type the lines objecting to an agreement will usually have an interpretation of the public interest or other standards which is consistent with their own interests, and this in itself should raise questions regarding the validity of the whole process.

The nature of these difficulties may be illustrated with reference to the problems faced by Japanese lines on the Pacific in recent years. From the commencement of container services on this route six Japanese lines operated in space charter agreements filed with the FMC covering Pacific south west, north west and New York routes respectively.

Through the 1960s and 1970s there were no great problems with renewals, although hearings were sometimes protracted. In June 1980 a further application was made prior to the impending expiration of the agreements in August of that year. The arguments in favour were that the space charter agreements reduced over-tonnaging and congestion at the ports. In January 1981 the FMC approved the application for three years, back-dating it to the previous August, but it made approval contingent upon limitations in the TEU capacity of that part of the service operated under slot charter arrangements. Following this four American carriers, APL, Sea-Land, Lykes and US Lines objected on the basis that the space charters are anti-competitive, and (in a curious echo of the case against the North Atlantic carriers) that the FMC did not approve them correctly. Although the agreements continue to operate they are under challenge in the courts. Whilst this was going on the Japanese carriers filed requests to replace old ships with substantially larger newbuildings, which would be of optimum size. This was again challenged by American lines who were already operating large ships themselves and, as independent operators do not require FMC approval for increases in their own capacity. In this way the regulatory regime itself may be exploited as a restraint on competition by lines ostensibly arguing on the basis of an anti trust standard.

In trying to find the source of many of these problems it is instructive to look back at the views of the Department of Justice itself on regulatory policy as expressed in the conclusion to its report on the Regulated Ocean Shipping Industry published in 1977. The Department first of all considered repeal of the Ocean Shipping Act leaving a completely unregulated industry subject both to the common law of common carriers and the anti trust laws. The first of these two Acts would then prevent discrimination between customers whilst the second would forbid conferences, pooling agreements, tying arrangements, dual rate contracts and predatory conduct. The Department was very much in favour of this as a matter of principle, but decided it would be impracticable because of the serious problems of comity which would arise from any attempt to mandate full anti trust liability for all shipping conferences serving US trades. It then considered the alternative of applying anti trust laws to US carriers only, allowing foreign flag firms to continue under the existing system. It approved of this as a partial solution but dropped the idea as it feared that it would leave US carriers vulnerable to predation from conferences and would be politically unpalatable. Having fairly quickly abandoned the idea of repeal of the Shipping Act it then turned to modifications which it considered would increase competition.

The first of these was the repeal of Section 14b of the Act which allowed dual rate contracts. If this could not be achieved the Department suggested that the dual rate system could be weakened by reducing the spread of rates from 15 per cent to 10 per cent, limiting the notice which shippers would have to give to release themselves from their contracts from ninety days to fifteen, reducing the level of liquidated damages and placing the burden of proof that the spread of rates was reasonable upon the carriers. Dual rate contracts would also be prevented completely from applying to inter modal shipments. The Department also suggested a change in Section 15 of the Shipping Act to codify and strengthen the Svenska test, the applicants to file agreements having to meet the following burden :

1. Prove that the anti competitive effects of the proposed agreement are clearly outweighed by substantial public benefits or serious transportation needs; and

2. Demonstrate that the goals cannot be met by alternative means having a lesser anti competitive impact.

A related proposal was that all dual rate contracts and anti competitive agreements under Section 14b and 15 should expire periodically and be discontinued unless they could be justified anew under the Svenska test, during which time past conduct would also have to be justified. (It is clear that a policy rather like this has been followed by the FMC in recent years with respect to the consortia agreements discussed above).   The report also favoured the right of independent rate action for lines within conferences and the prohibition of pooling agreements. Finally it argued for the abolition of the 'naturally tributary' theory for ports and the encouragement of inter modal freedoms, except of course for any lines using tying arrangements with shippers.

Given the tremendous difficulties there have been with the existing regime it is scarcely possible to imagine how the industry could have functioned under these proposed changes.   What is important about the Department of Justice report and recommendations is the simplistic view taken of the structure of the industry and operation of conferences (discussed at length in the UWIST Report for CENSA), the obsession with the idea of predation, and the apparent view that conferences must be considered guilty of anti competitive activity against the public interest and in contravention of other regulatory standards until proven innocent.   At the same time there is the readiness to contemplate an enormous burden of regulatory intervention and continuous monitoring in a system which would allow little more than weak rate agreements.   The attitude to dual rate agreements is particularly instructive, because if they could not be banned the Department of Justice clearly intended that they should be chopped to pieces by a detailed set of regulations with the remains being smothered in a blanket of argument about justification and degrees of relative anti competitiveness.

Most countries which have reviewed the operation of the conference system have made the broad judgement that on balance its operation was in the interests of the industry and the public good.   Then having prohibited certain anti competitive practices like the use of fighting ships, they have granted immunity against anti monopoly laws and left the industry to function without excessive regulatory monitoring. Where there are checks and balances they are usually provided by Shippers' Councils.   In 1961 with a set of comprehensive amendments to the Shipping Act, Congress tried to do much more than this and ensure that the conference system would operate in accordance with regulatory rules and standards embodying principles of equity and the public interest.   It was also its aim to produce a regime in which the US merchant marine would flourish.   Both of these attempts have failed. There has in fact been a synergistic relationship between the Shipping Act and the anti trust laws, the two working together to produce a regulatory regime of exceptional harshness.   The regulatory standards backed up by the anti trust laws impinge against many aspects of the normal functioning of the market and impose severe limitations upon the planning and operational procedures of carriers and particularly of consortia. The Act also deluded carriers into believing they had anti trust immunity, when in fact they had not, and because of the contradictory voices within the regulatory system there is a Catch 22 situation in which carriers can be positively encouraged to take actions for which they are later penalised. Further to this contravention of some of the detailed technicalities and cumbersome procedures of the Act came to be taken as offences against the anti trust laws themselves. Finally the sheer weight and cost of legal action and the use of the law as an element in competitive tactics came to represent an important distortion of the market. Thus as it evolved through the 1960s and 1970s the regulatory system developed into a legal quagmire which impaired industry function and the public interest, as weighed by the standard of common sense.

It may well be that any attempt to regulate industry function on the basis of broad standards, capable of wide interpretation and tested in the courts is doomed to internal contradiction and ultimate failure. Certainly the Department of Justices' own recommendations for increased regulatory supervision would have exacerbated all the problems of the 1961 regime. In the event the 97th Congress produced a movement for genuine reform, as will be discussed further in the next chapter.

The Issue of Comity

As has been demonstrated above the US operates a regulatory system of exceptional severity. At the same time it claims extra-territorial application for its shipping laws. This offends against comity (which may be defined as the friendly recognition by nations as far as practicable of each others laws and usages) as well as being of doubtful validity in international law.

The rules of substantive law which make up the American system are held to apply to agreements concluded in the US and carried out abroad and to those concluded abroad and carried out in the US. The application of this principle to shipping contracts concluded abroad was established in the case of US v Nordeutscher Lloyd 1912, whilst the reverse case was dealt with in US v Aluminium Co. of America 1944. As a result the US claims the right to legislate for acts and agreements made in foreign sovereign states, by carriers who may be nationals of those states, so long as the services covered have effects in US trades. It also claims the right to demand the production of evidence held abroad where it may relate to cases arising from the regulation of the liner shipping industry. As pointed out in the UWIST Report this extra-territorial reach of US laws applies to the anti trust laws as well as to the Shipping Act, exposing overseas nationals to the threat of prison sentences for actions which are considered to be perfectly legal in their own countries.

Under international law the domestic laws of one nation will apply in others only if the offence in question is agreed by the community of nations to justify violation of the strict territorial principle, and also if the constituent domestic and overseas component of the offence are legally entirely inseparable. Clearly in most cases offences under

US shipping law are not recognised as justifying a violation of the territorial principle. On the contrary in many cases there have been strong protests and some countries have enacted blocking statutes which render compliance with US law illegal in their own countries.

The UWIST Report concluded by recommending that if there were to be regulation of the international shipping industry it should only be on the basis of agreement between the states sharing the right to regulate the industry. Notwithstanding their general opposition to regulation of liner conferences they further recommended that :

> "the system of regulation should be certain and that all carriers subject to regulation should be able to determine their legal position: in particular they should not be subject to uncertain multiple actions under the Shipping Act and the anti trust laws. The Shipping Act should supersede the anti trust laws entirely as far as the international shipping industry is concerned. The substantive laws should be amended so as to permit conferences to organise their activities in the most efficient way."

The most severe problems of comity did not arise as a deliberate act of government policy, because if the Shipping Act had retained primacy of jurisdiction the penalties for violation would have been modest. However, deliberate or not, the problem of extra territorial application has become very serious and its implications with respect to international relations is one of the influences in the movement for regulatory reform.

Rationalisation and the Closed Conference System

The two major US routes the Atlantic and the Pacific have both suffered from over capacity, severe competition and rate wars. These problems have been attributed in large measure to the operation of the open conference system and European and Japanese lines have under the auspices of CENSA put forward a case for the European system of closed conferences and Shippers' Councils.

The early chapters of this book dealt in detail with the nature of competition in liner shipping and the case for closed conferences. The broad conclusion of this analysis was that the charge against the open conference system as the positive cause of over capacity cannot really be sustained, whilst by the same token the closed conference system would at best make only a modest contribution to the capacity problems of major US trades.

However, the fact that the closed conference system is not a panacea for the industry's ills does not in any way alter the case for the reform of what has become an arbitrary, internally contradictory, costly and harmful regulatory regime. Such reform, if it gave greater freedom to carriers to form consortia and to conferences to fix inter modal rates, would also improve operational efficiency and would help contain many of the pressures towards over capacity.

Other Issues

Two other issues emerged during the 1970s, the first concerned with the cross trading activities of the government controlled shipping lines of eastern bloc countries and the second with independents operating outside the jurisdiction of US regulation through the Canadian ports.

The activities of controlled carriers became an important issue not because of the extent of their competition in terms of market share, but because of the threat posed by lines which could operate on the basis of government subsidy and would not, therefore, be limited in their actions by the rules of the market place. This was a rather difficult subject because many American carriers themselves operate under subsidy. However, action was taken in 1978 when Congress passed PL 95 483, generally known as the Controlled Carriers Act. This amended Section 18c of the Shipping Act to give the FMC authority to disapprove the rates of controlled carriers operating to cross traders if their rates were found to be unjust or unreasonable. In this context the reasonableness of rates was defined in terms of their relationship to costs, and these could be either the quoted costs of controlled carriers, or their constructive costs, i.e. those of non controlled carriers operating similar vessels in the same trade.

The problem of the Canadian gateway was caused largely by the activities of CAST on the North Atlantic, which as a company operating through Canadian ports was not subject to the jurisdiction of the FMC and did not have to file its rates. This freedom was extensively used by the line in competitive rate setting which could not easily be monitored by other carriers. The issue was more tricky politically than that of controlled carriers because of the Pacific coast movement of Canadian cargo through US ports. A bill to control the Canadian gateway was, however, presented to the 97th Congress, whilst the proposals for new legislation also close this loophole.

10 The movement for regulatory reform

The regulatory regime of the US came during the 1960s and 1970s to work in a harsh and legalistic manner which interfered with the efficient functioning of the liner shipping industry, as well as raising serious issues of comity with trading partners. During this period many American carriers faced serious financial difficulties, and argued that they were at a competitive disadvantage to foreign lines, who could often shelter behind the blocking statutes of their governments. There is also a high level of subsidy of US carriers, and although some of this has been to support US shipyards rather than the shipping industry itself, the government has felt the need to try to reduce the overall level of support. As a result of these influences, together with the representation of foreign governments and carriers, a movement for regulatory reform developed in the late 1970s.

The movement took effect in the 96th Congress, when the House of Representatives produced its ambitious Omnibus Bill, covering almost all aspects of promotion and regulation for the maritime industries as a whole. Indeed the Bill was so broad in its coverage that it offended against a wide range of interests, and even those who approved of some of its provisions objected to others. It foundered in the face of general opposition, and was eventually stopped by the House Judiciary Committee. Meanwhile in the Senate the approach was to obtain a more limited measure of regulatory reform for the liner shipping industry alone. This was Mr. Inouye's Bill, which was in fact passed by the Senate, but was unable to complete the legislative process and lapsed with the ending of the Congressional term.

The initiatives for reform within the 96th Congress were unco-ordinated. President Carter did not have a policy and the separate parts of the administration spoke with conflicting voices. In particular the Department of Justice took a hard line against what it perceived to be the anti competitive activities of conferences, which was quite at odds with the view of Marad and even that of the Federal Maritime Commission itself. The approaches of the House and Senate were also far apart and since legislation requires that both pass an identical Bill, this substantially reduced the chances of success.

DEVELOPMENTS IN THE 97th CONGRESS

During the 97th Congress the approach was much more constructive. The Senate continued with its movement for regulatory reform in a new Bill 'S 1593', in which the lead was taken by Senator Gorton. Meanwhile, after adopting a low profile in the early part of the session, the House of Representatives came forward with Mr. Biaggi's Maritime Regulatory Reform Bill 'HR 4374', which was in many areas a mirror image of the Senate Bill and could have formed the basis of a ready accommodation between the two chambers. The Administration also tried to get its house in order and the Department of Transport (which had taken over Marad early in the Presidential term) produced a policy statement which was strongly supportive of Congress's efforts, although with one important qualification regarding tariff filing and rate enforcement.

The House and Senate Bills in the Spring of 1982

In their early form the two Bills represented a coherent view about the needs of the industry and (given twenty years of the operation of the old regime and the erosion of anti trust immunity) were based on an accurate understanding of legal technicalities and drafting requirements. Their major objectives were to improve the functioning and economic performance of the US Merchant Marine and the industry as a whole and resolve issues of comity. The method was to be the re-establishment of anti trust immunity together with the broadening of the operational freedoms enjoyed by carriers and conferences. In particular they intended to permit the easier formation of consortia and joint service agreements and the freer operation of inter modal systems. A related objective was to reform the regulatory process itself by speeding up and simplifying procedures for the filing and implementation of agreements, and limiting the time allowed for legal action. Finally specific reference was made to problems of comity, with the exclusion from regulatory supervision and the reach of anti trust laws of activities in foreign hinterlands, including the operation of Shippers' Councils.

Section 1 of the House Bill in March 1982 simply stated that it would replace the Shipping Act of 1916. Section 2 contained the definitions required for the workings of the Act, and although some of these were taken from the old Act there were a number of departures and important new terms. In particular there was a precise specification of the anti trust laws against which immunity was to be provided. The definition of common carrier was also broadened to include operations through ports in nations contiguous to the US, so bringing the Canadian gateway under regulatory supervision. Through transport and through rates were also defined in recognition of the need to deal with inter modal activities.

Section 3 defined authorised activities allowing ocean common carriers to agree to :

(1) discuss, fix, and regulate rates, including through rates, cargo space accommodations, and other conditions of services;

(2) pool or apportion earnings, losses, or traffic;

(3) allot ports or restrict or otherwise regulate the number and character of sailings between ports;

(4) limit or regulate the volume or character of cargo or passenger traffic to be carried;

(5)   engage in exclusive, preferential, or cooperative
       working arrangements among themselves or with one
       or more marine terminal operators or nonvessel
       operating common carrier;

(6)   enter into other agreements to control, regulate,
       or prevent competition among themselves; and

(7)   limit, in the case of conferences, membership.

Although Clause 7 of Section 3 allowed conferences to be closed if the
members so wished, it was made clear in Section 4 that conference agreements should allow any national line admission.   No provision was made,
however, for the Shippers' Councils usually associated with the closed
system.

Sections 4 and 5 concerned the filing and implementation of agreements.
Section 4 provided for virtually automatic filing for agreements that
complied with certain basic provisions, whilst Section 5 allowed for
implementation within 45 days.   In this way the FMC's authority was to
be confined largely to those cases where agreements were challenged,
subsequent to filing.   Where such a challenge was made, either by the
FMC or other complainant, a conclusion would be required within 180 days
or the case would lapse.   Further to this the burden of proof was placed
on the party opposing the agreement, which was to remain in force during
the case.

Section 6 of the Bill provided for loyalty contracts, permitting a dual
rate system, but without the need for a case by case approval by the
Commission and without the 15 per cent limit to the spread of rates.
Inter modal rates were also to be allowed, although in this case the
conference had also to offer the shipper an equivalent rate covering the
ocean freight only.

Section 7 of the Bill provided for anti trust immunity being drafted in
very broad terms as follows:

(a)   The antitrust laws do not apply to:

(1)   any agreement or activity described in section 3,
       whether or not filed under section 4 or effective
       under section 5, and whether or not exempted from
       any requirement of this Act under section 16;

(2)   any loyalty contract or any activity pursuant to
       that loyalty contract;

(3)   any activity prohibited by this Act or regulation
       promulgated under this Act;

(4)   any agreement or activity that relates solely to
       transportation services within or between foreign
       countries;

(5)   any agreement or activity with a shipper's council
       organized under the laws of a foreign country and
       operating exclusively outside the United States,
       including an agreement or activity that affects cargo
       transported in a United States import or export trade;

(6)   any agreement or activity to provide or furnish
        wharfage, dock, warehouse, or other terminal
        facilities outside the United States;

(7)   any agreement or activity with respect to the inland
        portion of any intermodal movement occurring outside
        the United States, though part of the transportation
        is provided in a United States import or export trade;
        and

(8)   any agreement, modification, or cancellation approved
        by the Commission prior to the effective date of this
        Act under section 15 of the Shipping Act, 1916 or
        permitted under section 14(b) thereof and any duly
        filed and published tariff rate, fare, or charge, or
        classification, rule, or regulation explanatory thereof
        implementing that agreement, modification, or cancellation.

Section 8 provided for tariff filing with the standard provision that
rate increases could not become effective within less than 30 days of
filing, whilst Section 9 dealt with controlled carriers continuing the
old law on the subject.

Section 10 which specified the prohibited Acts was to replace a number
of sections of the old Act.   Among the important prohibitions were any
form of rebating or departure from published tariffs, the use of fighting ships or predatory action against outsiders and unjust retaliation
or discrimination against shippers.   The public interest and detrimental
to commerce standards were, however, to be dropped.

Penalties were provided for in Section 13.   They were generally to be
modest compared to those of the anti trust laws, with civil fines not
exceeding US $5,000 for a violation of the Act or US $25,000 for a
wilful violation, each day of a continuing wilful violation constituting
a separate offence.   Penalties for rebating were to be more severe with
provision for suspension of tariffs, after which the use of a suspended
tariff was to be subject to a fine of US $50,000 per shipment.

The other provisions of the Bill were technical, covering the following
aspects:

    Section 11 Complaints, Investigations, Reports and Reparations
    Section 12 Subpenas and Discovery
    Section 14 Commission Orders
    Section 15 Reports and Certificates
    Section 16 Exemptions
    Section 17 Regulations
    Section 18 Repeals and Conforming Amendments
    Section 19 Effective Date

As stated above, in the Spring of 1982 the Senate Bill was rather like
the House Bill, the main difference being that conferences had to be
open and provision was made for Shippers' Councils.   The Bill also
made some provision for independent rate action and retained the maximum
spread of 15 per cent for dual rate contracts.

Under these Bills the attempt to reform the regulatory regime was
comprehensive.   First there was the precise specification of the anti

trust laws against which immunity was to be granted; second the granting of broad anti trust immunity for agreements coming within the scope of the Act; third the dropping of the public interest and detrimental to commerce standards and the replacement of the other standards with a more specific set of prohibited acts and finally, the complete revision of regulatory procedures. By this last provision the uncertainties inherent in the philosophy of the Svenska decision and the anti trust standard for the weighing of the public interest, which have become embedded in the procedures of the existing regime would have been dealt with. At first sight the Bills might have appeared excessively lenient, but given the enormous weight of regulatory intervention and procedural delay which have developed around the existing regime, this was necessary in the attempt to achieve genuine reform.

The activities to be authorised in Section 3 of the House Bill were not exceptional by the standards of other conferences around the world. But just as regulatory supervision worked synergistically with the anti trust laws to create a regime of exceptional severity, so the measures of reform outlined above would have provided substantial relief from the legal burden of the existing regime, and allowed much greater operational freedom, flexibility and opportunity for rationalisation.

ISSUES ARISING FROM THE BILLS

Tariff Filing and Rate Enforcement

Perhaps the most surprising of the issues of early 1982 was that of tariff filing and rate enforcement. It arose initially during the hearings on the Canadian Gateway Bill, when opponents suggested that the need for such legislation would disappear if the domestic regime were changed to do away with rate enforcement. This approach was taken up by the Administration as being in line with the President's view on the reduction of government involvement in the industry, and was supported by the Department of Justice as a means of maintaining a high degree of competition within the proposed new regime.

Tariff filing and rate enforcement were introduced only in 1961 as a means of implementing controls on the dual rate system, but they were at the heart of many of the most contentious issues of the regulatory regime, including the hugely expensive settlements made by the North Atlantic lines. Further to this in the European model of closed rationalising conferences, rate enforcement is a matter for conferences alone and policing arrangements are internal. In fact the Administration's stance on this was superficially close to that of the CSG countries, and large shippers also supported it. However, tariff enforcement is of much more importance for the relatively weak conferences of the US than it is for closed conferences; and shipping lines came out strongly in favour of the existing system. Some of them believed for a time that the Administration's recommendation was an attempt to torpedo the whole movement towards regulatory reform and would have preferred to do without a new Act entirely rather than accept it. There were a number of reasons for this. First, with a new Act as described above many of the problems connected with the operation of the present system would disappear. Violations of such an Act would not be contraventions of the anti trust laws, whilst the streamlining of filing and implementation procedures would remove the need to take chances. This would take the Catch 22 element out of regulation so that although penalties for wilful contravention would still be strong enough to make the system effective, they could be avoided by any line prepared to stick to the rules and take a minimum of care. On the other side tariff filing and enforcement has a number of positive advantages. First it enables conference lines to monitor the rates of independents. Second it places certain restrictions on the selectivity with which they can set rates by bringing them within the ambit of common carrier provisions. Third it provides a ready means of monitoring the rates of controlled carriers and of applying the principle of constructive costs to them. Finally it helps conference lines directly by buttressing internal policing procedures and providing a basis for withstanding pressures from large shippers. In fact with all the problems of the open conferences on US routes in recent years, rebating on the scale experienced on the Far East route is unknown, and this cleanness of rates is acknowledged to be a valuable feature of the system by many lines. Conversely, without the back up of rate enforcement by the regulatory regime, the US system might indeed be so weak as to lose all control of rates.

Independent Rate Action Within Conferences

Individual carriers have often asked for freedom of independent rate action, but this has usually been held to run counter to the whole basis of the conference system. As shown in Chapter 8 the problem has arisen in acute form in the last few years, particularly on the Pacific route, and the recent re-constitution of the Pacific conferences and rate agreements was only possible with some provision being made for 'Rate Initiative.' This is a form of independent action where, if the conference share of the market drops below 75 per cent of the total, lines have the right to set new rates: these then becoming available to all members.

Independent rate action is still strongly opposed by the more tradit-ional conference lines. Outsiders also dislike it as they see that it gives conference lines the possibility of selective response, which could possibly be co-ordinated to provide the equivalent of fighting ships. Technically this threat should be taken care of by prohibitions against predatory action, but this could require a costly court case and the provision of proof might be difficult.

Service Contracts

Large shippers have traditionally been characterised by something approaching total indifference to the questions of shipping regulation and anti trust immunity, and during the early hearings on the House and Senate Bills many of them were conspicuous by their absence. During the course of 1982 they did, however, find an issue which was of impor-tance to them, which was that of individual service contracts. This is said to have arisen following Du Pont's experience of individual negot-iations with the railways after the de-regulation of the Carter admin-istration.

Special service contracts do exist in certain trades, one of the notable examples being that of the Ford contract with Evergreen on the North

West Europe Far East route. They are characterised by the fact that detailed terms of service as well as rates are tailored precisely to the needs of a shipper. For example the line might make a number of containers available at a standard rate irrespective of what is in the box, thus simplifying documentation, whilst the availability of boxes and free time at shippers' premises could also be covered and could differ from standard terms. In the Evergreen Ford case the terms of the contract are confidential, as the contract is with an outsider on a route which does not have tariff filing and rate enforcement, and confidentiality also suits large shippers, as it helps to sustain a favoured position.

Where there are very large shippers common carrier provisions may not apply simply because the products moved are specific, and the volumes are so large that they affect operating costs, particularly in inland sectors. Nevertheless, taken together provisions for independent rate action and service contracts would change the character of conferences, eroding common carrier obligations to the trade as a whole in favour of closer attention to precise requirements of large shippers. In a regime where both exist there might also be a synergistic relationship between them, with individual conference lines using independent action to bid for the cargoes of large shippers on a service contract basis, in much the same way as outsiders.

Closed Conferences and Shippers' Councils

The question of closed conferences and Shippers' Councils i.e. of the European versus the US model was considered by many to be of equivalent importance to this issue of anti trust immunity itself. As mentioned in earlier chapters the case was put forward that closed conferences would provide for rationalisation, whilst Shippers' Councils would guarantee equity and the prevention of monopolistic abuse.

It was shown in Chapter 8 of this book that neither open nor closed conferences could guarantee rationalisation. However, the ability to form consortia does seem to be of great value as they provide a means by which a number of interested lines can participate in a route, in a service in which the operational pattern is rationalised, without the need for each of them to scale up to full size. On smaller routes this system allows for the organisation of the one or two rationalised services which are required, whilst on the large ones it may lead to the formation of a handful of major services which can rationalise by reaching a tacit accommodation between themselves and allowing space for fringe and inter modal operators.

In fact during the course of negotiations there was a move from some major lines away from the position in favour of closed conferences. This arose partly because of the realisation that this was one of the less important aspects of regulatory reform as well as being difficult to get through Congress. There were also certain fears that adoption of the closed system would substantially narrow the gap between US law and the provisions of the UN Code and if the US later acceded to the Code without reservations, cargo sharing would become applicable to US trades. US carriers are in favour of this, as it would increase their market share in many trades, and some provision for cargo reservation was included in the Omnibus Bill. It has also been suggested that cargo

sharing could provide an attractive off budget solution for the
Administration to the problems of the US Merchant Marine.   This threat
might have seemed to be fairly remote, as accession to the Code by the
US would be fraught with difficulties.   However, in the Summer of 1982
the issue of protectionism arose directly in the form of an amendment
to the House Bill to allow US carriers to operate in markets where the
Code and other forms of cargo reservation apply.   This will be discussed
further below.

The issue of Shippers' Councils has always been of relatively little
importance in the US, partly because of problems with anti trust legislation and partly because the large shippers are not really interested,
preferring to aim for a system of service contracts.   Provision for
them was made in the Senate Bill, at a time when it was fairly close to
the European model and allowed closed conferences, and this remained in
the Bill even when the clause in favour of closed conferences was
dropped.

Developments in the Summer of 1982

Both House and Senate Bills had made good progress by the Spring of 1982
and there appeared to be a fair chance that they might pass into law in
a form fairly close to the original.   However, in the middle of the
year progress slowed.   The Senate Bill became bogged down when Senators
Thurmond and Metzenbaum refused to allow it to go through on the consent
calendar and threatened to filibuster if it were presented on the
discussion calendar.   This would have taken up a great amount of
precious time so the Bill was held for a while in a state of limbo.
Meanwhile the House Judiciary Committee decided to take a look at the
Biaggi Bill, although stopping short of the full hearings which almost
inevitably would have spelt its doom.   In this process the Bill,
although accepted as a measure for the shipping industry, was examined
to see that it did not move the balance of power away from shippers to
an unacceptable extent.   During this time there was a gathering of
forces opposed to the Bill.   Some of these were special interest groups
like ports who feared that they might have something to lose from the
inter modal freedoms provided within it;   but there was also an anti
trust group opposed to the Bill on ideological grounds and this included
the Department of Justice who as guardian of the anti trust laws, now
began to increase its pressure against the new legislation.

Opposition to the Bills found public expression in July 1982, immediately
following the distribution of a report by the General Accounting Office
on the state of the US Merchant Marine.   This report was issued after
some four years of investigation, and the timing of its release at the
precise point in time when the House Judiciary Committee was looking at
the Biaggi Bill, was suggested by some to be more than coincidence.   The
report seemed innocuous enough, pointing out that the decline in the
number of ships in the general cargo sector was to some extent an inevitable concomitant of containerisation and suggesting that, in the liner
sector at least US carriers had a reasonable share of domestic trade.
However, it was used as a focus of attention by the national press in
an attack of the two Bills.   Thus on the 12th July the Washington Post
took up the line of the GAO Report, reiterating the point that the US
Merchant Marine was not in such decline as had been thought, and crit-
icising anti trust exemptions, which it held would increase costs to

consumers.   On the 14th July the New York Times quoted a calculation
by an American maritime economist Allen Ferguson, in which the provision of anti trust immunity and recovery of rate control by conferences was estimated to increase freight rates by some 20 per cent, or
US $3 billion per annum, of which US $2 billion was estimated to go to
foreign lines.   Finally on the 15th July the Wall Street Journal took
up arms, in this case concentrating on subsidies, but also arguing that
anti trust immunity would not help much in an industry suffering from
over capacity as a result of excessive subsidisation around the world.
In spite of the brevity of these articles, and the naivety of some of
the views expressed, they did touch common chords of chauvinism, concern
over the high level of subsidy and suspicion of cartels, and encouraged
the House Judiciary Committee in its search for safeguards to run alongside the provision of anti trust immunity.   The content of the negotiations which took place during this period is clearly not available to
an outsider, and the situation was for a while so fluid and changed so
rapidly that it would in any case be impossible to follow it in any
detail.   However, when the Biaggi Bill was eventually released by the
Judiciary Committee it had undergone a number of significant changes.

THE BIAGGI BILL ON PASSAGE THROUGH THE HOUSE

The Biaggi Bill was finally marked up and released by the House
Judiciary Committee in the late Summer.   It came to the floor of the
House in mid September where it was passed by an overwhelming majority.
The Bill retained the same basic objectives and structure as the earlier
version discussed above, and the provisions for tariff filing and
enforcement remained unchanged, but in many other areas there were
important differences.   First in Section 3 the provision for closed
conferences was dropped, this being a return to the traditional approach
of the US trades and consistent with the Senate Bill.   At the same time
provision was made for the setting up of neutral bodies for the internal
policing of conference agreements and some form of provision was made
for Shippers' Councils, although their status vis a vis the anti trust
laws was not very clearly defined.

Sections 4 and 5 retained the simplified procedures for filing and
implementation of agreements but in Section 4 provision was made for
independent rate action.   This was completely unconstrained, being
stated in the following terms:

(1)   Each conference agreement must provide that, if
        the conference has in effect a loyalty contract
        with one or more shippers, each member of the
        conference may take independent action on any rate
        or service item contained within a tariff required
        to be filed under section 8 whenever -

        (A)   a member requests the conference to amend
                a rate or service item and announces its
                intention to take independent action if the
                conference does not agree to the amendment;

        (B)   the conference fails to make the proposed
                amendment within thirty days after the first
                consideration of the amendment in a conference
                meeting;   and

        (C)   the member seeking the amendment requests
                    the conference to include in the conference
                    tariff a separate entry for its account as
                    proposed in the amendment.

  (2)   The agreement must further provide that, if the require-
        ments of paragraph (1) are met, the conference shall
        include the proposed amendment in its tariff for use by
        any member of the conference and that the amendment shall
        become effective on publication and filing, but no later
        than forty-five days after the initial request.

In Section 5 there was a modification of the 180 day guillotine on
legal action, two further periods of 90 days becoming available provided that:

    "there is a reasonable probability that upon further invest-
    igation the Commission would find that the agreement would
    operate in violation of this Act, or
    a shipper, common carrier, or marine terminal operator is
    likely to be substantially injured after the agreement is
    allowed to go into effect before a final decision on its
    merits."

Section 6 on loyalty contracts re-imposed the maximum spread of rates
of 15 per cent but was otherwise unchanged.

Section 7 still provided for broad anti trust immunity.   There were
some changes in drafting which reduced the breadth of coverage although
these seemed to be designed to prevent sins of commission, and would
not have placed too many difficulties in the way of lines trying to
abide by the rules, as would certainly have been the case for most of
them.

Section 8 retained the previous tariff filing provisions, but allowance
was made for time volume rates and also for service contracts.   This
important provision was drafted as follows:

  (c)   SERVICE CONTRACTS - An ocean common carrier or conference
        may enter into a service contract with a shipper to provide
        specified services under specified rates and conditions,
        subject to the requirements of this Act.   Each contract
        entered into under this subsection shall be filed confid-
        entially with the Commission, and a concise statement of
        its essential terms shall be filed with the Commission
        and made available to the general public in tariff format,
        and such essential terms shall be available to all shippers
        similarly situated.   The essential terms shall include -

      (1)   the origin and destination port ranges in the
            case of port-to-port movements, and the origin
            and destination geographic areas in the case of
            through intermodal movements;

      (2)   the commodity or commodities involved;

      (3)   the minimum volume;

      (4)   the line-haul rate;

(5)   the duration;

(6)   service commitments; and

(7)   the liquidated damages for non-performance,
      if any.

The exclusive remedy for a breach of contract entered into
under this subsection shall be an action in an appropriate
court, unless the parties otherwise agree.

Section 9 on controlled carriers was unchanged but in Sections 10 and
11 dealing with 'prohibited acts' and with 'complaints, investigations,
reports and reparations', there were important changes.   The main ones
were at the start of Section 10 where it was stated in Paragraph (a) (1)
that

"Subject to paragraphs (2) and (3), no common carrier,
directly or indirectly, may form a joint venture with other
common carriers operating in the same trade if such conduct
substantially reduces competition in the trade considered as
a whole

(2)   Paragraph (1) shall not apply .... if such conduct

(A)   results in gains in efficiency or services
      that outweigh any diminution in competition;

(B)   is required by the express provision of a
      government to government agreement;   or

(C)   is in furtherance of foreign policy interests
      of the United States which outweigh the interests
      of the United States in preventing a substantial
      reduction in competition.

(D)   Permits US flag carriers to carry cargo of the
      importing or exporting foreign state which would
      otherwise be unavailable to such carriers, or
      available only on unequal terms by reason of the
      cargo reservation laws or trading practices,
      government or otherwise, of such states, provided
      that the agreement is not unjustly discriminatory
      against US carriers."

The first point about this is that it re-introduced the principle of
justification for joint service agreements.   Of even more importance
was the fact that in C and particularly in D provision was made for
joint service agreements in protectionist or cargo sharing environments.
In such an environment a joint service agreement is of course a carve
up of the trade, shutting out competition completely.   There was also
a hidden sting in the tail when it became clear that American carriers
might claim that accession to the UN Code of Conduct for Liner Conferences was prima facia evidence of cargo reservation, providing justification for invoking this clause.   With many of the major European
nations about to accede to the UN Code this caused great concern.   As
will be discussed below in Chapter 11 the accession to the UN Code is
with the reservations contained in the Brussels Package, which confine
its application to trades between developed and developing countries
only, and even in this limited context allow the lines of the developed
nations on a route to re-negotiate their shares, so as to get away from

the strict confines of 40:40:20. Further to this the strict interpretation of the UN Code deals with conference shares only, and in
principle the conference has to win its cargo rather than having it
reserved. However, the threat or protectionism in the US was considered sufficiently serious for the General Council of British Shipping
to refer to it in their annual British Shipping Review, which usually
confines itself to rather less contentious issues. The Review drew
attention to the threat of protectionist policies in the US, re-affirm-
ing the commitment of British lines to the multi-lateral philosophy of
the Brussels Package and re-stating their faith in its efficacy. The
changes of Section 10 were repeated in Section 11. But this section
deals only with complaints and investigations so that the clauses have
a defensive rather than an offensive impact. A final change in the
Bill took the form of a new Section 18 which provided for the setting
up of a Commission on the De-regulation of International Ocean Shipping
with the following functions:

   (c)   COMMISSION FUNCTIONS - The Commission shall conduct a
comprehensive study of, and make recommendations
concerning, the deregulation of international ocean
shipping by common carriers. Such comprehensive study
shall specifically address -

      (1)   various options for deregulation of the
international ocean shipping industry, with
reference to their ability to promote an
efficient, stable, and competitive United
States common carrier fleet;

      (2)   the opportunities for harmonizing United
States policy toward international ocean
shipping with the policies of our major
trading partners;

      (3)   the system for determining tariffs based on
the classification of goods and its role in
a future deregulated industry; including the
most effective method for eliminating unnece-
ssary cargo classifications as a basis for
establishing tariffs and the feasibility of
establishing a single tariff by each conference
or common carrier for all cargoes shipped in
units of comparable size, weight, and handling
characteristics.

      (4)   the role of the antitrust laws in the inter-
national shipping industry and their impact
upon our relations with foreign nations;

      (5)   the impact of the "rules of competition" being
considered by our trading partners and their
relationship to the trend in the developing
world towards structured cartelization;

      (6)   the impact deregulation may have on the growth
of State-owned or State-controlled merchant
fleets;

> (7) the size of the United States liner fleet,
> by number and cargo capacity, which each of
> the deregulation options may produce; and
>
> (8) the future structure and role of the Federal
> Maritime Commission in a deregulated industry.

Some of the changes discussed above were relatively minor.   These
include the switch to open conferences and the restriction of the spread
of dual rates to 15 per cent, which are features of the existing regime
that conferences already live with.   They were also part of the Senate
Bill even in the Spring of 1982.   The weakening of anti trust cover and
extensions of time available for legal action were considered by the
guardians of the anti trust philosophy to be important safeguards, but
they might not have caused too much difficulty because most carriers try
to stay within the law, and the simplification of rules and procedures
would have made compliance much more straightforward.   The Bill still
provided anti trust immunity for conferences and extended this to
operating consortia and inter modal rates.   It also retained tariff
filing and rate enforcement to support the integrity of conference price
structures.

There were three potentially important problems with the Bill in the
form in which it passed the House.   First, certain of the provisions
like those for independent rate action and customised service contracts
could have provided a ready made Trojan horse within the conference camp,
allowing loyalty contracts and conference rate structures to be under-
mined from the inside.   Second, the changes in section 10 would have
weakened the basis of regulatory simplification, returning to a process
of justification in terms of relative degrees of anti-competitiveness,
which harks back to the public interest standard and the Svenska test.
At the same time, in a contradiction which is typical of the existing
regime, this provision could have opened the way for bilateralism on a
scale previously unknown.   Finally, as changes multiplied and the Bill
became more untidy the possibility increased that it might lead to a
spate of clarifying litigation, which as well as being costly, could
again undermine anti trust immunities and the attempt to simplify
regulatory procedures.

The Senate Bill failed to reach the floor by October the 1st 1982 when
Congress recessed.   A final effort was then made for the lame duck
session in December.   This concentrated on the Biaggi Bill as time
would have been to short to allow for passing of the Gorton Bill,
followed by a conference and the final passing of identical Bills.
For a time prospects seemed to be quite good, particularly as the
Administration continued to provide support.   There was a final mark
up of the Biaggi Bill in which certain of the problem clauses were dealt
with and an accommodation was made with the Senate Bill.   Attempts were
made to find a slot in the Senate timetable, and if it had come to a vote
the Bill would almost certainly have passed, in spite of a further attack
on it by the New York Times.   In the event it failed to reach the floor
and lapsed with the closing of the lame duck session on the 22nd December.

The movement for reform could continue in the 98th Congress with an
early re-introduction of the Biaggi Bill, but there will inevitably be
new elements in the political scene in 1983 and prospects must at best
be rather uncertain.   There are also proponents of an alternative policy

concentrating on direct measures for the promotion of the US Merchant Marine which might be allied to the growth of bilateralism. The failure of a movement for reform which would allow conferences to function in an environment which contained a large measure of competition to be replaced by protectionist policies which would directly limit competition, would be a severe setback reducing long term prospects for international harmony and the efficient evolution of the liner shipping industry. It is, therefore, to be hoped that the proponents of reform will gather their forces for a further attempt at legislation.

11 The UN Liner Code, CENSA Code and EEC competition rules

HISTORICAL DEVELOPMENT

The debate about the regulation of liner conferences in the US was only part of a world wide process. The other major arena was UNCTAD, including within this the meetings of the CSG countries and of CENSA who took a major part in the debates of UNCTAD and produced their own Code of Conduct for liner conferences along the way.

The negotiations of UNCTAD were fundamentally different from those of the US because they were not primarily concerned with the operation of the market place and its relation to a theoretical competitive ideal. During the UNCTAD negotiations there was fierce criticism from some of the developing countries of conferences, but these were still accepted as a fundamental feature of the liner trades and were in fact made the vehicle for the achievement of developing country aspirations. Given this as a starting point the debate focussed on two main issues, first, the share of national flag carriers in the trades of their own countries and second, the relationship between shippers and conferences, particularly with respect to negotiations over freight rates.

Although the UNCTAD process proper started in 1964 there had been a number of earlier moves. In the developing world some countries began to implement policies for the development of national fleets by the unilateral process of cargo reservation; whilst in Europe, following problems between shippers and conference lines, discussion between the two sides produced a 'note of understanding' which allowed for the setting up of an independent panel to resolve those disputes which could not be dealt with in direct negotiations.

In 1964 the first UNCTAD conference took place in Geneva with the objective of promoting and fostering the economic advance of less developed countries by means relating to trade. One of the supporting studies dealt with maritime transport and among its proposals was one for the international regulation of shipping conferences. Two courses of action were recommended for further study, one of which was based on legislation and the other on the adoption of an international statute of conferences as a collective measure of self discipline. The policy making continued at a conference in Algiers in 1967 where the developing countries met at Ministerial level in the 'Group of 77', and asked that in preparation for the full UNCTAD meeting of 1968 the shipping committee should consider international legislation. In this meeting their particular pre-occupations were confirmed as the level of freight rates, which were still held to be discriminatory against the exports of developing countries, and their right to develop national fleets via conference membership.

The outcome of the second UNCTAD conference in New Delhi in 1968 was a compromise between the views of developing and developed nations and was embodied in a resolution that member governments, and particularly those of the developed maritime nations should ask conferences to take account of the following possible courses of action.

a. To review and adjust, if necessary, freight rates which shippers and other interested parties in developing countries consider to be high, bearing in mind the importance of as low a level of freight rates for the traditional exports of developing countries as is commercially possible;

b. to provide special freight rates for non-traditional exports in order to promote the expansion of the trade of developing countries;

c. to avoid freight rates set at levels which cannot be justified by the normal criteria for freight rate structures, and also conference practices which will have the effect of frustrating the export of a product from a developing country in order to encourage the export of the same product from another country served by the same conference;

d. to recognize port improvements leading to a reduction in the costs of shipping operations for the purpose of reviewing and adjusting freight rates as appropriate;

e. to make suitable arrangements for authoritative representation of the liner conferences in the ports of developing countries served by them;

f. to make their tariffs and other relevant notices available on request freely to all interested parties.

There was also a recommendation that governments should invite the liner conferences to admit as full members the national flag lines of those developing countries which were their trading partners.

During the second UNCTAD the division into four groups took place, group A representing Afro Asian countries, group B the developed market economies, group C South American countries and group D the centrally planned countries of Eastern Europe. Following this groups A and C began work with the UNCTAD Secretariat on a Code of Conduct to replace the rather weak recommendations of New Delhi. At the same time there was a West European initiative for conference self regulation. In the UK the Rochdale Committee of enquiry recommended that "members of conferences should collectively adopt a published code of conference practice which would contain provisions relating to the admission of new members, the publication of tariffs, the provision of information about revenues and costs to representatives of the government and of shippers, and consultation with the government and shippers".

In February the Ministers of the countries of the Consultative Shipping Group met in Tokyo for further discussions to produce a group B response for UNCTAD and agreed that it was essential that there should be a Code of Conduct. Such a Code was duly produced under the auspices of CENSA in November 1971 and officially accepted by the governments of the CSG countries.

In early 1972 groups A and C agreed upon common proposals and at the third UNCTAD meeting in Santiago the debate focussed around the CENSA Code and alternative developing country proposals. The Santiago meeting also set up a preparatory meeting to draft a universally acceptable code and during 1973 there were a number of meetings in Geneva where the alternative Codes were compared and an attempt was made to resolve the differences between them. Agreement did not prove possible, first because of the cargo sharing provisions of the developing countries and second because of some of their legal provisions which the lines considered to be unworkable.

Nevertheless, at a Plenipotentiary conference held in Geneva in 1974 the UN Code was promulgated by a vote of seventy two to seven, with five abstentions. All the countries of groups A, C and D voted in favour, whilst the group B countries were badly split, some supporting the Code, others opposing it and some abstaining.

Under Article 49 of the Code it was to enter into force six months after the date at which not less than twenty four states (the combined tonnage of which amounted to 25 per cent of the world total as measured in 1973) became contracting parties. This required the support of at least some of the major shipping nations of group B. It appeared likely to be forthcoming in 1975 as West Germany, France and Belgium announced the start of ratification procedures, these of course being countries whose national lines stood to gain by the adoption of cargo reservation procedures on routes between the developed nations themselves. However, the Commission of the EEC challenged these independent initiatives arguing that the Community as a whole had to decide jointly on the basis of accession, and as a consequence in 1976 all EEC countries agreed to negotiate a joint formula. For a while negotiations were deadlocked, but in February 1979 under the provisions of the Brussels Package, agreement was reached on a compromise formula which allowed for accession with reservations. Shortly after this other Western European countries and Japan also announced plans for acceding to the Code thus guaranteeing its entry into force. This is now expected sometime in 1983. During the 1970s the US official line was firmly opposed to the Code, which runs almost precisely counter to the domestic philosophy for the regulation of liner shipping. However, in the early 1980s as the movement for regulatory reform gathered momentum in the US, and entry into force of the Code became imminent, it became the subject of study and debate.

PROVISIONS OF THE CODE

The two basic provisions of the UN Code are embodied in Articles one and two, the first providing for conferences to which the national lines have the right of membership and the second for the reservation of cargo for national lines. Under Section 3 of Article 1 it looks as if third flag carriers have a fair opportunity to enter the conference under criteria similar to those traditionally employed by closed conferences, viz :

(a) The existing volume of the trade on the route or
routes served by the conference and prospects for
its growth;

(b) The adequacy of shipping space for the existing
and prospective volume of trade on the route or
routes served by the conference;

(c) The probable effect of admission of the shipping
line to the conference on the efficiency and
quality of the conference service;

(d) The current participation of the shipping line in
trade on the same route or routes outside the
framework of a conference; and

(e) The current participation of the shipping line on
the same route or routes within the framework of
another conference.

But this is clearly modified by the cargo reservation provisions of
Article 2. Section 4 of this article states :

"When determining a share of trade within a pool of
individual member lines and/or groups of national
shipping lines, the following principles regarding
their right to participation in the trade carried by
the conference shall be observed, unless otherwise
mutually agreed:

(a) The group of national shipping lines of each of
two countries the foreign trade between which is
carried by the conference shall have equal rights
to participate in the freight and volume of traffic
generated by their mutual foreign trade and carried
by the conference;

(b) Third-country shipping lines, if any, shall have the
right to acquire a significant part, such as 20 per
cent, in the freight and volume of traffic generated
by that trade".

Thus the 40:40:20 rule is stated flexibly. It confers rights rather
than duties and provision is made under further Sections of Article 2
for re-allocation of traffics where national shipping lines are
unavailable or unable to carry a full 40 per cent, and for re-distrib-
ution of shares among the lines at one end of a route by mutual agreement. Although cargo sharing is based in the first place on revenue
pools within the conference, this is backed up by the provisions of
Sections 12 to 15 of Article 2 that the lines at one end of a route may
require that a pool be instituted. There is also the fall back
position that in the absence of a pool cargo sharing may be based on
"sailing arrangements which provide the same opportunities for national
lines as if pools did exist". Article 3 of the Code on decision
making procedures changed the nature of Conference decision making by
giving national lines a right of veto :

"The decision-making procedures embodied in a conference
agreement shall be based on the equality of the full
member lines; these procedures shall ensure that the
voting rules do not hinder the proper work of the conference and the service of the trade and shall define the
matters on which decisions will be made by unanimity.
However, a decision cannot be taken in respect of matters
defined in a conference agreement relating to the trade
between two countries without the consent of the national
shipping lines of those two countries".

Articles 7 to 11 of the Code cover relations with shippers, including
loyalty arrangements, conference reports to Shippers' Councils and
consultation between shippers and conferences.   In these areas the UN
Code is close to CENSA following the principles of the COAR conference.
Under Section 2 of Article 11

"The following matters, inter alia, may be the subject
of consultation:

(a)   Changes in general tariff conditions and related
        regulations;

(b)   Changes in the general level of tariff rates and
        rates for major commodities;

(c)   Promotional and/or special freight rates;

(d)   Imposition of, and related changes in, surcharges;

(e)   Loyalty arrangements, their establishment or changes
        in their form and general conditions;

(f)   Changes in the tariff classification of ports;

(g)   Procedure for the supply of necessary information by
        shippers concerning the expected volume and nature of
        their cargoes; and

(h)   Presentation of cargo for shipment and the require-
        ments regarding notice of cargo availability."

Articles 12 to 17 deal with the important matter of freight rates.
Article 12(a) states that :

"Freight rates shall be fixed at as low a level as feasible
from a commercial point of view and shall permit a reasonable
profit for shipowners."

Article 13 contains the provision similar to that of US law that conferences should not unfairly differentiate between shippers similarly
situated whilst Article 14 holds that a conference should give 15 days
notice of freight rate increases.   Rate increases are also to be
subject to negotiations with Shippers' Councils and in accordance with
the principles of the COAR system, such negotiations are to be based
on independently verified data on costs and revenues.   In Article 14
the Code departs from the COAR system as generally practiced in that on
failure to reach agreement the matter has to be submitted to international conciliation.   But although this arbitration is mandatory
acceptance of the results is not, and in the absence of acceptance by
carriers Section 6 of Article 14 states :

"Shippers and/or shippers' organizations shall have the
right to consider themselves not bound, after appropriate
notice, by any arrangement or other contract with that
conference which may prevent them from using non-conference
shipping lines.   Where a loyalty arrangement exists,
shippers and/or shippers' organizations shall give notice
within a period of 30 days to the effect that they no longer
consider themselves bound by that arrangement, which notice
shall apply from the date mentioned therein, and a period of
not less than 30 days and not more than 90 days shall be
provided in the loyalty arrangement for this purpose."

Whilst under Section 7 :

"A deferred rebate which is due to the shipper and which
has already been accumulated by the conference shall not
be withheld by, or forfeited to, the conference as a
result of action by the shipper under article 14, paragraph 6."

Article 15 of the Code provides for promotional freight rates, the
justification for this being provided by shippers, whilst Article 16
deals with surcharges to cover sudden or extraordinary increases in
costs of loss of revenue, and Article 17 makes provision for a currency
adjustment factor.   Article 18 prohibits the use of fighting ships and
Article 19 reiterates the requirement for adequacy of service.   The
first part of the Code then concludes with some minor technical provisions.   Part 2 of the Code deals with mandatory conciliation procedures and with provisions for implementation, entry into force and review.

ISSUES ARISING FROM THE CODE

Much of the early debate on the Code was concerned with its impact on
world trade and economic development in the third world.   In commenting
on the issues in 1974 Deakin concluded that conferences could not be a
source of subsidy or aid.   He also found that conferences do not act
unfairly against developing countries, the discrimination in their
pricing policies being against the higher value goods which are typically the exports of developed countries.   He was in favour of developing country participation in liner shipping, although aware of the
complexity of operations and the need to build up inter-linked conference memberships to obtain proper fleet deployment.   His views on rates
and the inclusion of public utility standards to avoid the distortions
of monopoly have been discussed in an earlier chapter, but arrangements
of this nature were not incorporated into the Code;   they were almost
certainly unworkable and would have run directly counter to cargo
sharing provisions.

Other aspects of the debate were concerned with the possibility that
strict implementation of cargo sharing provisions would lead to excessive fragmentation in shipping services and a reduction in average ship
size to below the economic level.   Against this Sturmey argued that
cargo sharing was a right and not a duty and that developing countries
would use it sensibly.   He also argued that there would be general
economic benefits from the increase in developing country participation
in world liner shipping, (as the developing countries had a comparative

advantage in this industry) and there would be general improvements in efficiency arising from a lessening of monopoly powers which would result from the processes of consultation embodied within the Code. (The Future of Liner Shipping, 1976).

Most of the thinking on which the Code was based related to the age of conventional break bulk shipping. In reviewing it from the standpoint of container shipping and of competition and regulation in the late 1970s and early 1980s a number of additional issues arise which have not yet received much attention.

PROVISIONS OF THE CODE AND ECONOMIC EFFICIENCY

Although conferences as envisaged by the Code are not technically identical to those of the COAR system, they are similar in many respects, and the Code is based on the implicit assumption that they will have substantial market power. The regulation of conference activities then becomes the prime means by which developing country aspirations are met, and it is assumed that rationalisation within the conference will automatically mean that services are provided efficiently.

In Article 1 of the Code cross traders are considered and criteria for their possible entry to the conference are set out, but no mention is made of outsiders. Following this in Article 2, rights to participation refer specifically to cargo carried by the conference and not to the trade as a whole. There was, however, a powerful statement made by India on behalf of the Group of 77 following promulgation of the Convention. This pointed out that the Group of 77 agreed to the provision of the Code on the limitation on fighting ships and supported the participation of independents in a trade on the clear understanding that "non conference shipping lines would not be permitted to operate in a manner which damaged the smooth functioning and operation of liner conferences." The statement went on to refer to the apprehension of the Group of 77 regarding outsiders and stated that operation of non conference lines should not be allowed to erode the provision regarding the share of national flag carriers. It also stated that should a situation arise in which national lines began to lose market share, governments would have full freedom of action in the national interest to ensure that independents operated on a commercial basis in fair competition. In practice this may easily mean trade wide cargo reservation or the banning of independents. Some developing countries have already taken such action and are unlikely to change it upon entry into force of the Code.

The analysis of earlier chapters showed that on any liner route there may be pockets of low cost capacity available from the operation of flexible ships, which may economically be made available at less than the conference rate, whilst the use of land bridge and trans-shipment techniques may allow new routes to be used outside the conference which also provide low cost capacity. It has further been shown that there may well be a viable outsider strategy on a route, and outsiders have often provided an important stimulus for change when conference lines have been caught by changes in prices or technology which make them uncompetitive. For these reasons conferences cannot guarantee that they will maintain for national lines an 80 per cent share of the market. In order to maintain such a share it may be necessary to back up the conference with measures to suppress competition.   In this way the natural evolution of the industry may be stifled in taking up one apparently easy option for gaining market share.

There is within the Code an alternative theme regarding outsiders which reflects shippers' interests.   Thus fighting ships are banned and access to independents competing upon a fair and reasonable basis is commended. Further to this in the event of breakdown in price negotiations and the subsequent mandatory conciliation procedures, the final recourse is to independents, via the release of shippers from their contractual obligations without loss of any outstanding deferred rebate.   These provisions of the Code are completely at variance with the general thrust of cargo sharing provisions and are probably meaningless.   They suggest a possible recourse to competition to protect shippers' interests when the general regime envisaged by the Code is one in which rationalising conferences have control of the market.   This contradiction was perhaps inevitable in a set of negotiations which attempted to cover the interests of both lines and shippers.   But it is clearly impossible to obtain the benefits of competition and the advantages of price competition provided by outsiders in a regime whose over-riding objective is to obtain the development of national lines by means of the operation of conferences, backed up if necessary by techniques of cargo reservation.

The Code may appear to provide a flexible framework within which signatories will act sensibly, as argued by Sturmey.   But its basic philosophy lends itself readily to protectionism of a type that closed conferences have not known and, if provisions for conference control and cargo reservation work, it must be subject to the dangers and costs associated with this.   These dangers may be particularly acute where the developing countries are high cost operators, and this could paradoxically give participating lines from the developed countries easier opportunities for profit than are usually available to them.

COVERAGE OF THE CODE

Although the main aim of the Code was to allow developing countries to realise their aspirations, it was drafted in general terms as a universal document for the regulation of the liner shipping industry.   When one examines the structure of world trade it can be seen that traffic between developed countries is substantially larger than that involving developing nations.   Further to this in the trades between the developed countries themselves the shares of national lines are not precisely aligned with flows of cargo, and the application of cargo sharing would require a tremendous re-organisation, operating to the benefit of national lines which have so far been relatively unsuccessful and to the detriment of the successful national lines and cross traders.   This would run counter to the long held traditions of these trades and also to the general principles of multi-lateralism in trade on which the growth of group B countries has been based.   The possible stresses which could arise from this were brought into focus in the very early stages with the split in attitude towards the Code of the group B countries.   In fact accession to the Code has been made with reservations which limit its breadth and also its scope.   Right from the start group D countries and many of the Group of 77 stated that the Code would not apply to those trades which were covered by inter-governmental agreement,

these being handled on the basis of bilateral negotiations.   In 1979 in
the Brussels Package, the Council of the EEC made a number of important
reservations, as the basis on which member countries should accede to
the Code.

Annex 1 of Council Regulation 954/79 states :

"When ratifying the Convention or when acceding thereto
Member States shall enter the following three reservations
and interpretative reservation :

1.   For the purposes of the Code of Conduct, the term
       'national shipping line' may, in the case of a
       Member State of the Community, include any vessel-
       operating shipping line established on the territory
       of such Member State in accordance with the EEC Treaty.

2.   (a) Without prejudice to paragraph (b) of this reser-
            vation, Article 2 of the Code of Conduct shall not
            be applied in conference trades between the Member
            States of the Community or, on a reciprocal basis,
            between such States and the other OECD countries
            which are parties to the Code.

       (b) Point (a) shall not affect the opportunities for
            participation as third country shipping lines in
            such trades, in accordance with the principles
            reflected in Article 2 of the Code, of the ship-
            ping lines of a developing country which are
            recognized as national shipping lines under the
            Code and which are :

            (i)   already members of a conference serving these
                  trades;   or

            (ii) admitted to such a conference under Article 1
                  (3) of the Code.

3.   Articles 3 and 14 (9) of the Code of Conduct shall not be
       applied in conference trades between the Member States of
       the Community or, on a reciprocal basis, between such
       States and the other OECD countries which are parties to
       the Code.

4.   In trades to which Article 3 of the Code of Conduct
       applies, the last sentence of that Article is interpreted
       as meaning that :

       (a) the two groups of national shipping lines will
            coordinate their positions before voting on matters
            concerning the trade between their two countries;

       (b) this sentence applies solely to matters which the
            conference agreement identifies as requiring the
            assent of both groups of national shipping lines
            concerned, and not to all matters covered by the
            conference agreement. "

Thus the Brussels Package reserved major trades between developed nations from the cargo sharing provisions of the Code, and also allowed EEC nations trading with the developing countries to re-distribute their own shares. When it comes into force the Code will apply mainly to trades between developed and developing countries, excluding of course those of the US. Coverage is clearly severely limited, compared to that envisaged when UNCTAD set out to draft a universal document. In one way, however, the effects will still be quite widespread, because it looks as if some conferences will have to be re-organised to form coherent groups according to whether or not member countries have acceded to the Code. There are also fears that the Brussels Package might not hold and, as a result, the industry will drift into a generally protectionist era, and these have been acutely felt with respect to the possible policies of the US.

The US Position

The one large remaining issue concerning the likely coverage of the Code relates to the possibility of US accession. The official position as stated by the US representative to the Plenipotentiary Conference in 1974 was as follows :

"A.   The membership provisions encourage the continuation of closed conferences. In this regard, Mr. President, it is ironic that the closed conference system, which was so bitterly attacked by developing countries throughout most previous UNCTAD shipping meetings, is now sanctioned on an international scale by those same developing countries under the auspices of UNCTAD.

B.   The cargo-sharing provisions will cartelize the transportation of trade. Such provisions subordinate trade to transport; they restrict the choice of shippers and may result in delay of shipments and consequent loss of trade.

C.   The provisions on freight rates freeze them for unduly long periods, which could strangle the liner industry. Rate rigidity will hurt shippers as much as carriers."

Meanwhile US shipping lines conscious of their own relatively low share of trade compared to the 40 per cent allowed in the Code have generally been in favour of accession without reservations; although in most cases they prefer straight bilateralism, which allows them more easily to by-pass the provisions of their own regulatory regime.

Although the process of regulatory reform in the US could narrow certain of the differences between the domestic regime and that of the Code they would still be substantial. Closing the gap so that the US could accede to the Code which would then replace the current regime or a new shipping Act of the form discussed above, is a process which could hardly be imagined. However, the US under the present regime has had to learn to trade with those of its trading partners which employ cargo reservation techniques, the necessary accommodations have been made, and the results have been reasonably to the liking of US carriers. As discussed in Chapter 10 a similar accommodation was made in the later stages of the Biaggi Bill, first as a defensive measure in Section 11, and then ostensibly as a tidying up exercise in Section 10, where it has offensive

potentialities.   In this way cargo reservation and protectionism could
come to US trades and the threat is not nearly as remote as might be
imagined.

A NOTE ON EEC COMPETITION RULES

For many years the EEC did not have a specific policy for the liner
shipping industry and the negotiation of the Brussels Package was the
first major development in this area.   However, in 1981 a draft set of
regulations concerning the application of EEC competition rules to liner
conferences was prepared by the Commission and circulated to member
governments for comment.

The background to this was set out in an explanatory memorandum to the
draft regulations which reviewed the legal position.   This referred to
a judgement in the Commission v French Republic 1974 in which the Court
of Justice upheld the Commission's view that, although sea and air transport were not covered by provisions relating to the common transport
policy until such time as the Council decided to include them, "nevertheless they were on the same basis as other modes of transport, subject
to the general provisions of the Treaty."   In a further judgement in
the Commission v Belgium 1978 it was confirmed that these general provisions of the Treaty should in particular include the competition rules
embodied in Articles 85 and 86.   However, under Council Regulation No.
141 of 1962 it was stated that Regulation No. 17 of 1962, which was the
first implementing Articles 85 and 86, did not apply to transport.
Further to this the later Regulation No. 1017/68 of 1968 applied the
competition rules only to transport by rail, road and inland waterway
and this left sea and air transport as the only branches of the economy
where the competition rules did not apply.

Pending entry into force of such rules, Articles 88 and 89 of the Treaty
of Rome provided the legal basis for action by member states of the
Community.   Under Article 88 the authorities of member states "shall
rule on the admissability of agreements and on abuse of a dominant position in accordance with the law of their country and with Articles 85 and
86."   Whilst Article 89 requires the Commission in co-operation with the
authorities of member states to investigate infringements and propose
measures to bring them to an end.

The Commission argued that the position prevailing in 1981 presented the
risk that there would be a succession of independent legal judgements
within member states which would not be coherent or take sufficient
account of the needs of the industry.   The draft regulations were then
presented.   They were fairly straightforward, providing immunity to
Article 85 for joint service agreements and conferences.   However, they
did make some suggestions with respect to the nature of the loyalty
contract, which was to be breakable if the conference could not provide
adequate service.   Article 86 on predatory conduct still applied leaving
conferences open to the suspension of agreements for relatively minor
infringements.

In the UK the Select Committee of the House of Lords on the European
Community decided to hold hearings on this subject.   In the first of
these the Department of Trade gave evidence and put forward the view

that the loyalty contract should apply to only 70 per cent of the total of each shippers' cargo, the rest being available to outsiders without loss of rebate.   In the second hearing evidence was presented by the General Council of British Shipping.   Among the points made by the GCBS was that concerning the dangers of the clash of jurisdiction between alternative regulatory regimes.   In this respect it pointed out that the UN Liner Code and Brussels Package were about to come into effect and suggested that they should be allowed to settle down before any new rules were applied in this sector.   It also argued that clashes of jurisdiction with the regulatory regime of the US could take two decades to resolve and from the analysis of the above chapters on the US legal regime, this seems to be no exaggeration.   A further major point made by the GCBS concerned the proposal of the Department of Trade with respect to loyalty contracts.   This it argued was absolutely unworkable involving in principle a scrutiny of shipments made by each shipper to see that the 70 per cent rule was complied with.   The basis of this would also be difficult to determine as it could apply to either weight, measurement or freight value, and if the latter to either sea freight or the through movement.

It is still early days with respect to the proposed competition rules and the eventual outcome of the Commission's initiative can hardly be anticipated at this stage.   However, as presently drafted they would represent a significant change, which would add to the problems of conferences both directly, via changes in the loyalty contract and rules relating to the misuse of a dominant position, and indirectly through prospective clashes with other regulatory regimes.

12 Summary and Conclusions

In drawing together the main conclusions of this book the approach will be to start with the historical perspective, moving on to market and conference function and finally, to regulation and policy issues.

HISTORICAL PERSPECTIVE

Conferences came into being in the late 19th Century shortly after the development of an economic and reliable steamship made liner services possible. At that time shipowners needed to combine to obtain the scale for frequent and regular services, this requirement for scale constituting a barrier to outsiders at a time when there was a strong tendency towards over capacity. As they developed into powerful cartels conferences naturally became the subject of dispute, and this led during the early years of this century to a number of official investigations of conference function. In their evidence to these enquiries conference lines made the case that the only alternatives to the conference system would be either chaotic markets, unable to maintain price stability or provide the required quality of service, or monopoly. This case was accepted by the Alexander Committee in the US (whose recommendations led to the Shipping Act of 1916) and also by the Royal Commission on Shipping Rings in the UK. This set a general trend and as a result conferences were given immunity from anti trust laws in developed nations. They then controlled most liner markets throughout the rest of the conventional era.

In the early years of containerisation many conferences appeared to be even stronger than before. This was first because of the increase in scale required for the operation of a weekly service, second because the new container lines and consortia were able to start with a clean sheet and third because they gained a head start on the competition. But some container routes like the North Atlantic were quite competitive right from the start and competition became more widespread and intense towards the end of the 1970s.

There were a number of reasons for this growth in competition. First there has been in the post war years a massive increase in the availability of finance for shipping ventures, which began in the oil and bulk trades and later spilled over into liner shipping. This has been supported by the fact that many of the largest container lines are now subsidiaries of conglomerates which themselves have substantial resources. Governments too have taken an interest and have supported new national lines with a variety of measures from fiscal aids to direct financial involvement and subsidy.   Further to this, it has in recent years been possible to obtain new ships on very favourable terms, this being largely the result of government support for shipbuilding industries in a depressed world market.   As a result scale has proved not to be an insurmountable barrier to competition.   In particular the newly industrialising nations of the Far East have successfully developed a number of major new lines.   They have had a number of particular advantages, being situated in an area of great financial strength and trade growth and having access to two of the four large trade routes of the world. They have also taken advantage of cheap crews and of changes in the cost mix in the mid 1970s which left the established lines with ships which were much too fast.   Most of the lines of the newly industrialising countries developed in the mid and late 1970s, concentrating on the Pacific and the Europe Far East routes.   There have, however, been other areas of growth, and Hellenic, which is a private company, is making a substantial investment, whilst US Lines, which is also privately owned, is contemplating the construction of 14 giant containerships which would add substantially to world capacity.   This is despite the weak container markets of the early 1980s.

In certain other more technical ways the scope for competition increased in the container era.   First, although containerisation plus the growth of specialised bulk carriers cut the old tramp ship out of liner markets, this form of competition re-surfaced in a new form with the development of the flexible ships described in Chapter 3.   Although this has not been particularly important in terms of the total capacity provided, it is a difficult form of competition to counter, being based on pockets of low cost capacity.   More important than flexible ships was the more extensive use of inland transport in inter modal networks.   This led directly to a new form of outsider competition in the form of the land bridge, of which the Trans Siberian Railway is the most important example.   The rather less dramatic use of inland modes in mini bridges tends to increase inter conference competition as well as offering new scope for outsiders.   Finally, the use of land transport in combination with absorption pricing systems has made it possible for lines to compete widely within a conference area whilst serving only a limited number of ports, this also increasing competition among conference lines and offering extended scope for outsiders.

Competitive pressures built up in the late 1970s with increasing supply coming up against weakening demand and also changes in the balance of flows brought about by fluctuating exchange rates – particularly the decline of the US dollar.   By 1980 all of the three large conference routes were in a state of disarray, losing control of rates and suffering from over capacity, although the extent of this varied depending upon the precise circumstances of the route.   For a time it looked as if the whole system was under threat and certain of the major groups were considering the possibility of its evolution into one in which large lines and consortia would act outside the conference framework. However, by the Summer of 1982 this possibility seemed to have receded as both on the Pacific and the Europe Far East route the conferences regained control and began to institute rate recovery programmes. Further, in spite of the vociferous criticisms made by shippers and the tough bargaining which often takes place with conferences, they still support conference lines, even when there are reliable alternatives which are competitive in terms of price.   Thus the conference system still appears to fulfill a need in spite of all the challenges of recent years and all the problems it has faced. To consider this further one must turn to the question of conference function.

COMPETITIVE CHARACTER AND CONFERENCE FUNCTION

Much of the argument about conference function took place in the mid 1970s as part of the movement to achieve regulatory reform in the US. At this time the well known closed conference routes from Europe to Australasia, South Africa (which was just in the process of being containerised) and the Far East were all relatively strong, whilst the North Atlantic, as one of the largest and longest established open conference routes, often had a tempestuous time. When the two systems were compared the closed conference in its idealised COAR form was put forward as the best possible system for the industry and clear way ahead, whilst the open conference was frequently criticised as the worst of all possible worlds and positive cause of over capacity. These arguments were supported partly by the evidence cited above and partly by models of closed and open conference function described in Chapter 6 and based on Chamberlin's fundamental work on the theory of monopolistic competition.

The criticism of these ideas is also based partly on evidence (in this case updated to take account of the experience of recent years) and partly on an analysis of conference function. The main criticism of the earlier models is that they do not take account of the competitive character of container systems, and in particular of the differences in character between routes. An alternative approach was developed by extracting from the early chapters on ship type, size economies and the nature of inter modal systems, a set of parameters by which the competitive character of container routes could be evaluated. The first and most important of these is the traffic volume of the route in relation to the capacity of a fleet of ships of optimum size, itself a function of route length. Fleet capacity is some 150,000 TEUs per annum with medium size ships and double this with third generation ships of 3,000 TEUs. When these basic capacities are set alongside figures of throughput on world routes it becomes clear that only a very few of them will sustain more than one or two weekly services. These are the Pacific, the Atlantic and the routes from Europe to the Far East and Middle East. They are all competitive, with competition tending to become more intense as route length diminishes. In contrast the small routes which will sustain only a very limited number of full scale services have all been much less competitive. However, route size and length are not the only dimensions, there is also the fringe based on the flexible ships and alternative route patterns described above. The potential for competition in these areas depends upon an entirely different set of characteristics viz. cargo mix and transport geography. Finally, given the general tendency in the modern world for nations to wish to develop their national fleets, the degree of alignment between cargo and market shares must be a factor affecting the potential level of new entry.

The analysis was taken further in Chapter 7 by consideration of the relationship between parameters of competition, the market share required for entry on routes of varying character and the decision to enter. Following this a review of container routes encompassing about

one half of deep sea container capacity in 1980, illustrated the relationship between route character and the nature of competitive action.
Thus the routes from Europe to South Africa and Australasia were shown to be fundamentally less competitive than the Pacific, Atlantic and Europe Far East routes and the success of their conferences owes as much to this as it does to the closed system. Similarly, the review of the three large routes shows that by 1980 they were all highly competitive and even the FEFC could not hold on to the rationalised position of its early years. It was also shown that open conferences are not routes where open entry is combined with price maintenance; on the contrary prices have been savagely cut in recent years and although this leads to some rationalisation it does not always seem to prevent new entry. On the other side, in the closed conferences the barriers to entry are now not as strong as they once were and new national lines in particular have been able to obtain entry to the FEFC. Thus the case against the open conference as the positive cause of over capacity falls down, whilst by the same token the closed conference system is shown not to be a panacea. This in turn focuses attention on the more fundamental influences leading to disequilibrium in world markets, including the weakening of the growth of demand and more particularly the subsidisation of supply.

The collapse of the early 1980s does not by itself constitute an argument against the conference system, as it is difficult to see how any form of market organisation could have avoided a partial failure given the nature of the influences at work during this period, and the distortions arising from subsidised supply. But it does raise questions concerning the precise role of conferences in the modern world which must now be addressed.

On the relatively less competitive routes which will support only one or two services of optimum scale and do not offer much scope for competition from fringe operators, conferences may still operate broadly according to the principles of the COAR system. In this system conference control of rates and of entry is combined with operational integration in the form of a consortium or joint service agreement, which provides the scale required for efficient rationalised operations. The conference may of course have to leave some space for outsiders offering fringe competition but although this may put it under some pressure this is unlikely to be very severe. On routes of this size it is also possible to maintain relatively large differentials in rate structures, prices for certain commodities being reduced to encourage them to move, whilst the increase in scale or improvement in cargo balance achieved by such a policy can ensure that this takes place without detriment to higher rated goods.
Where routes have limited scope for competition, Shippers' Councils also perform their most valuable function, providing a forum for the airing of complaints and for negotiation over rates; whilst rules relating to rate negotiation which may require the provision from the lines of independently verified accounts can in principle constrain the misuse of monopoly power. Even so, this system is unlikely to provide the powerful stimulus to the search for efficiency which results from a serious competitive threat.

On the large routes, which will sustain a number of services of full scale, plus competition from flexible ships and alternative route structures the position is very different. These tend to attract competition simply because of the scope offered by their size and diversity.

Within such conferences, scaling up to economic size and the development of efficient operational patterns is a matter for the individual service rather than the conference and here the ability to form consortia and make joint service and slot charter arrangements is of crucial import- ance.   In these circumstances the joint service, as well as allowing operational optimisation, will accommodate a number of interests without the need for each of them to try to scale up to economic size, thus ameliorating tendencies towards over capacity.   A joint service arrange- ment will substantially reduce the level of competition between members and a consortium may even eliminate it, but by allowing the group of lines to be more efficient it could well increase the strength of comp- etition with other services as well as improving overall efficiency.   On large routes the joint service takes over a part of the function of a conference but since it is not route wide it can not achieve an overall capacity rationalisation on the route.   For this to be achieved there needs to be an accommodation, first between the conference members and second between the conference as a whole and outsiders, the outsider element consisting in this case of both fringe and service oriented lines.

In the closed conference the attempt is made to achieve the rationalis- ation of conference capacity by direct negotiation of market shares, whilst in the open conference this can not take place because there is no control of entry.   But the two systems contain the same elements and just as in the closed conference the failure of negotiations on shares can lead to price warfare, either in the form of rebating, or members leaving the conference, so in the open conference rate wars can lead eventually to a tacit accommodation on capacity and market shares.   It is not possible to make a once and for all choice between these two methods.   This depends on a wide range of circumstances, including the character of the route, the quality and technical character of operations at any given time, and the attitudes of shippers - particularly with respect to their tolerance of strong tying arrangements.   There may be certain circumstances where there are measurable gains from the approach of co-operative rationalisation and others where a route would appear to require a strong dose of competition.   All that can be said is that if competition or the threat of it is cut out of the market place it will eventually stultify.   The case can be made that the combination of rationalisation and competition allowed by moderately strong conferences operating in an open environment, represents a good method of maintaining progress.   In this approach the joint service agreement provides the basic capability for operational rationalisation and some limits to the growth of capacity, and this can be supported by various other features of the conference like tariff filing and enforcement etc., whilst service oriented outsiders and fringe operators maintain the pressure for change.

Open and closed conferences are variations on a theme and both can work so long as the pressures upon them are not excessively great and the competing lines all have to obey commercial principles.   From the evidence of Chapter 8 it seems that they need to be able to maintain a market share of about 75 per cent for the system to hold together.   This allows room for both fringe operators and also for one service oriented independent.

The other major aspect of conference function concerns rate making and in particular the complex structure of rates.   As explained in Chapter 6 conference rate structures vary by commodity, partly in response to costs, but also to some extent as a result of the varying elasticities of demand for transport. With the development of inter modal transport a new dimension was added as the conference rate was extended to encompass port and inland transport costs. This provides such scope for variation in response to detailed differences in cost structures or the application of pricing principles, that where there is more than one operator in the market there is no way that individual rate making could avoid a mass of anomalies. These would affect flows which in turn would affect costs in a process of continuous flux. Whether or not this would eventually settle down is arguable, but if it did it would almost certainly be by the use of much cruder structures than now exist. Coherence in rate structures in this complex environment does require a process of negotiation and this in turn helps in the development of the stable operational patterns which are a crucial element in the control of costs. In this respect it is interesting to note that many outsiders set their prices simply by discounting the conference rate structure and those that do not often work with a very simplified system of box rates.

Coming to the conditions necessary for effective conference function, the crucial requirements are the ability to negotiate, fix and police rates, including inter modal rates, whilst member lines need to be allowed to form consortia or operating clubs. To maintain the integrity of the conference, provisions for independent rate action and service contracts are best avoided. Immunities from anti-monopoly laws need to be complete, whilst any safeguards relating to conference function should take the form of clear cut prohibitions. This last provision is particularly important as attempts to ensure conformance with broad regulatory standards, capable of wide interpretation, tend to lead to excessive regulatory intervention, costly litigation and possibly to an eventual paralysis in decision taking.

Provided that the conditions set out above are satisfied the rest of the system does not have to be restrictive. In particular conferences may be open and tying arrangements relatively weak. In a system of this type there would be rationalising and co-operative forces at work but there would also be scope for competition and the eventual competitive structure would depend on the character of the route as described in Chapter 7 and illustrated in Chapter 8.

REGULATORY POLICY

In concluding the argument of this book the objective is to bring together the various threads in the development of regulatory systems and comment on the issues raised.

Figure 12.1 below sets out the major landmarks in the development of conferences and regulatory systems and distinguishes three main periods. The first of these was that of the formation of conferences in the late 19th Century and their operation into the early 20th Century when they came under government scrutiny. Following this the second period runs from the second decade of the 20th Century (when conferences were given their immunities from anti monopoly laws) until the late 1950s. Although there were two main systems operating during this period, (the US open conference and the European closed conference) when looked at from the perspective of the present day the differences between them seem to be relatively minor.   The third period runs from the late 1950s to the present day, and it has been during this time that major differences have developed between regulatory systems.

The first big change was in the United States which developed the system of positive regulation described in detail in Chapters 9 and 10.   Apart from the problems it caused in the operation of the industry this led to serious divisions between nations, and trading partners had to take measures to protect their national lines.   There has been another smaller element in the US system which has been the policy of allowing bilateral deals with developing countries.   This practice now seems likely to increase, notwithstanding the movement for regulatory reform and criticism in the US of both the UN Liner Code and the Brussels Package.   In Europe and the rest of the CSG countries a freer evolution of the industry (under the traditional anti monopoly immunities) has been allowed.   This led from the closed conferences of the conventional era to the consortia of the container age, which together with the conferences themselves and Shippers' Councils now make up the components of the COAR system.

The third major development was that of the UN Liner Code which took one decade to negotiate and another to reach its present stage of impending entry into force.   The main objective of the Code was to assist in the growth of the shipping industries of developing countries and the development of their trade, but it also set out to counter bilateralism and government intervention in developing countries and become a universal instrument of self regulation for the liner shipping industry as a whole.   It is still too early to judge the effects of the effectiveness of the Code in facilitating trade and economic development, but it is clear that it has not become the universal instrument that it set out to be, and is adding to further to the process of division in the regulatory systems of the world.   The CSG countries did of course play a major part in the negotiations in UNCTAD which led to the form- ulation of the Code, and are generally acceding to it, although trying to prevent it from extending to trades between the developed countries.

As a result of the developments outlined above there may now be considered to be a fourfold breakdown of regulatory systems - EEC/CSG, UN Liner Code, US multilateral and US bilateral, and in all sectors prospects are now very uncertain.   First, the UN Liner Code is about to enter into force, and in spite of all the time that has elapsed since its promulgation there is still some uncertainty as to its ramifications. In the US the situation is even more difficult to read.   There is still the possibility that there will be a new Shipping Act in the 98th Congress and even if this does not come about, there are likely to be some changes in the legal regime together with major changes in policy designed to support the domestic Merchant Marine.   Finally, in Europe discussions are now being held on a new set of prospective competition rules, whilst the CSG countries and the US are just about to enter into discussions on the problems of bilateralism.

PERSPECTIVES AND POLICIES

Three major problems facing the world of liner shipping today have been

Figure 12.1

The Evolution of Regulatory Regimes

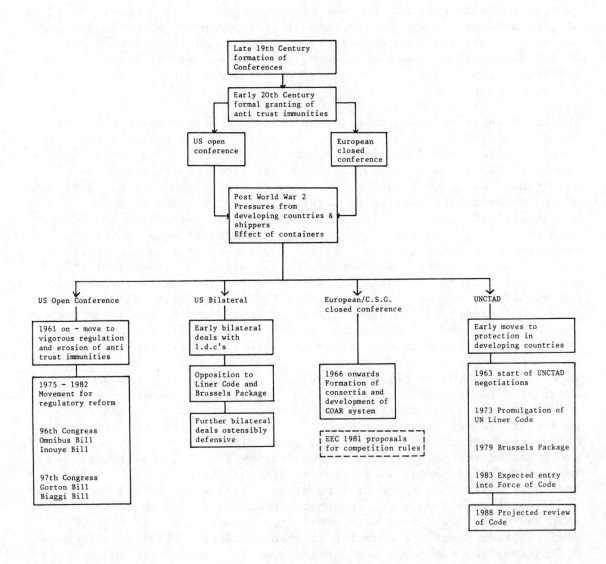

discussed.   These are first the general weakness of markets and the tendency towards over-supply, second, the aberrations of regulatory intervention and the growing divisions in the regulatory systems of the world and third, the growth of protectionism and bilateral dealing.

On the question of the weakness of markets there is not much that can be said.   No early resumption of growth in deep sea container trades is in sight and it is worth re-emphasising the points that the industry is of limited size, growth rates from the early explosion of the container revolution are now inevitably slowing down and there are close limits to the amount of capacity required.   On the supply side subsidy is the serious problem, although no easy solution to this is in sight.

Coming to regulatory regimes, the crucial issue in the world today is that of regulatory reform in the US.   In spite of disputes about it and the somewhat messy state of the final version of the Biaggi Bill in the 97th Congress, it is still a potentially constructive development of great power.   If eventually passed it would create a new form of regulated open conference, which could operate flexibly and efficiently in the container age, whilst leaving adequate scope for competition. Further to this it would resolve many of the issues of comity and make it easier for the US and CSG systems to come together.   In this respect the EEC initiative of 1982 appears ill-timed, whilst its apparent objective of harmonisation within the Community is excessively narrow. In reality the regulatory changes embodied in the EEC competition rules (certainly those of the first draft) would not be a simple harmonisation of existing immunities, but would bring about fundamental changes in pricing structures and conference operation.   Article 86 of the Treaty on misuse of a monopoly position is also to be interpreted by the Commission, an approach which carries with it all the dangers which exist when regulations are not clear cut.

Turning to the UN Liner Code there must be serious reservations about cargo sharing rules and their possible extension from a conference-wide to a trade-wide basis.   Protectionism is not confined to the Code as the less successful fleets in the developed world would also like to see cargo sharing, whilst increasing over supply could generalise this to all fleets except those of the major cross traders.   There could be some localised short term rationalisation from the development of protected routes, but even with cargo reservation this is not certain and there are tremendous hazards.   First, changes in regulatory regimes which present sudden new opportunities to particular lines and offer them protected markets, often encourage the purchase of new tonnage as opposed to the piecemeal acquisition of existing ships: and in the present context of world markets this could exacerbate the global problems of over capacity.   Second, barriers to entry are not necess- arily absolute and the question of entry is likely to become a political one.   Third, where officials control cargo allocations there must necessarily be a potential for beaurocratic delay and corruption. Fourth, cargo reservation does not prevent the errors of judgement, or changes in demand or the cost mix, which lead to over capacity and the operation of inappropriate tonnage.   Indeed, as the ultimate anti competitive policy, it is likely to weaken the drive for management efficiency and the effectiveness of the response to changing circum- stances.   Finally, in the container age protectionism may not always be effective in its immediate aims as alternative routes may develop to circumvent the rigidities of any reserved route which becomes too inefficient. Examples of this have already been seen in certain developing countries, where the continued operation of very inefficient conventional systems has led to the development of overland routes from neighbouring countries or even to the increasing use of air transport.

Coming back to the Code itself one wonders how necessary it was to have an international instrument in order that developing countries should increase their participation in the liner trades, as they were in any case finding their way into conferences. Cargo reservation itself may well be a blind alley inhibiting the freedom, flexibility and imagination with which the developing countries approach the intermodal era. There will be an opportunity for a change of direction in the review conference which should be held five years after entry into force in 1988, but for anything constructive to emerge and be implemented in a reasonable time would require an unusual consensus between developed and developing countries.

Looking at the issues which have been raised in regulatory policy in the last few years two scenarios can be defined which represent the opposite extremes. In the first (which is conference oriented and multilateral), the movement for regulatory reform would succeed early in the 98th Congress, whilst EEC competition rules would be delayed for a while and re-drafted to allow the EEC and a reformed US regime to work in harmony. Finally, the combined US and EEC/CSG regimes working together would restrain the tendency towards cargo reservation and bilateralism in developing country trades, and there would eventually be some movement towards the easing of cargo reservation in the UN Liner Code. The second scenario is government oriented and protectionist. In this the movement towards regulatory reform in the US would be blocked, and this would be associated with a lurch towards protectionist policies, European competition rules would be implemented as presently conceived and would exacerbate the differences between the US and EEC/CSG systems, and the developing countries would take a hard line in implementing the Liner Code associating with it policies of trade-wide cargo reservation.

In a world controlled by these latter developments, governments would intervene much more directly in liner shipping by the negotiation of cargo rights and the provision of subsidy for national lines, whilst protectionist/bilateral regimes would become much more important. In what remained of the multilateral sector conferences would wither leaving control in the hands of consortia and the large individual lines. Although existing loyalty contracts might be reduced in strength they would be likely to be replaced by individually negotiated contracts, whilst common carrier obligations would be generally eroded. The industry would continue to function, but this is in many respects an unattractive scenario, it would not leave much scope for competition but there would be no guarantee that it would avoid problems of over capacity. Indeed the regime bears some relation to the international airline business which is beset by such problems.

There is a national third case envisaged by supporters of deregulation. As discussed at the start of Chapter 9 it is difficult to know precisely what this is supposed to mean in the liner shipping industry, which is not a regulated one in the usually accepted sense of the term. If it means the removal of all forms of anti-monopoly immunity, it is also

difficult to see how it could come about, if only because of the
problems of comity which would arise in any piecemeal approach and the
strategic and other considerations which persuade governments that they
require national fleets. For all the criticisms that have been levelled
at it, the conference system still provides a convenient, flexible and
well tried method for operation of the liner trades. It has scored
some notable successes in recent years with the containerisation of
major routes, and is capable of further adaptation. Finally, although
it is a system which restricts certain forms of competition, it does
not shut it out of the market place and indeed most major routes have
been intensely competitive in recent years. The conference system is
under attack from protectionist policies, those in pursuit of a
deregulated utopia and shippers looking for short term bargaining
advantages. Only if there is support from shippers and governments for
its constructive evolution under regulatory regimes of a sensible nature,
which can operate in harmony with each other, will it continue to
function and serve the needs of trade and economic development.

Bibliography

Structure of the General Cargo Sector: Ship Choice

B.M.L. Business Meetings Ltd., Proceedings of Ro-Ro Conferences,
  B.M.L., Rickmansworth, Herts. 1976-81.
Buxton, I.L., Daggitt and King, J., Cargo Access Equipment for Merchant
  Ships, E & F Spon Ltd., London 1978.
Fearnley's (Annually) Review & World Bulk Trades, Fearnley's, Oslo.
Gilman, S., Ship Choice in the Container Age, Marine Transport Centre,
  University of Liverpool 1980.
Maritime Transport Research, Dry Cargo Ship Demand to 1985, Vol. 6,
  distributed by Graham and Trotman Ltd., London 1977.
The Marine Transport Centre, University of Liverpool, Container
  Logistics and Terminal Design. Distributed by the I.B.R.D. 1982.

Ship Size and Speed

Caracostas, N., Containership Economics for Effective Decision Making
  Analysis, American Society of Naval Architects & Marine Engineers
  1971.
Carreyette, J., Preliminary Ship Cost Estimation, Royal Institute of
  Naval Architects 1971.
Gilman, S., Maggs, R., and Ryder S.C., Containers on the North Atlantic,
  Marine Transport Centre, University of Liverpool 1977.
Ryder, S.C., and Chappell, D., Optimal Speed and Ship Size for the Liner
  Trades, Marine Transport Centre, University of Liverpool 1979.

Transport Geography

Gilman, S., and Williams, G.F., The Economics of Multi Port Itineraries
  for Large Containerships, Journal of Transport Economics and Policy,
  Vol. 10, No.2. 1976.
Gilman, S., Maggs, R., and Ryder, S.C., Containers on the North Atlantic,
  Marine Transport Centre, University of Liverpool 1977.
Gilman, S., Port Location and Cargo Flows in Container Systems,
  Symposium on Unitised Cargo Terminals, National Technical University,
  Athens 1979.
Pearson, R., Containerline Performance and Service Quality, Marine
  Transport Centre, University of Liverpool 1980.
Pearson, R., and Fossey, J., World Deep Sea Container Shipping, Gower
  Press 1983.

Competition on Liner Routes

Pearson, R., and Fossey, J., World Deep Sea Container Shipping, Gower
    Press 1983.
See also market reports in Containerisation International, Seatrade
    Shipping Magazine, Cargo Systems, Fairplay Shipping Weekly, Lloyds
    Shipping Economist and Lloyds List.

Liner Conferences (History and Function)

Bennathan, Esra., and Walters, A.A., The Economics of Ocean Freight
    Rates, Praeger, New York 1969.
Bryan, I.A., Regression Analysis of Ocean Freight Rates on Some Canadian
    Export Routes, Journal of Transport Economics and Policy, Vol. 8, No.2
    1974.
Chamberlin, E.H., The Theory of Monopolistic Competition, Oxford
    University Press 1949.
Davies, J., The Economics of the Open Conference System, Maritime
    Policy and Management, Vol. 7., No.2. 1980.
Deakin, B.M., and Seward, T., Shipping Conferences, Cambridge University
    Press 1973.
Devanney, J.W., Conference Rate Making and the West Coast of South
    America, Journal of Transport Economics and Policy, Vo.9, No.2. 1975.
Evans, J.J., Liner Freight Rates Discrimination and Cross Subsidisation,
    Maritime Studies and Management, Vol.4, No.4. 1977.
Evans, J.J., Concerning the Level of Liner Freight Rates, Maritime Policy
    and Management, Vol.9, No.2. 1982.
Heaver, T.D., Inbound Outbound Freight Rate Controversy, Centre for
    Transport Studies, University of British Columbia 1973.
Heaver, T.D., A Theory of Shipping Conference Pricing and Policies,
    Maritime Policy and Management, Vol.1, No.1. 1973.
Laing, E.T., The Rationality of Conference Pricing and Output Policies,
    Maritime Policy and Management, Vol.3, Nos. 2 & 3 1975/6.
Moore, K.A., The Early History of Freight Conferences, The National
    Maritime Museum 1981.
Shneerson, D., Structure of Liner Freight Rates, Journal of Transport
    Economics and Policy, Vol.10, No.1. 1976.
Sletmo, G.K., and Williams, E.W., Liner Conferences in the Container Age,
    Macmillan, New York 1981.
Sturmey, S.G., Shipping Economics (Collected papers), Cox and Whyman,
    London 1975.
Zerby, J.A., and Conlon, R.M., Liner Costs and Pricing Policies,
    Maritime Policy and Management, Vol.9, No.3. 1982.

Liner Conferences (Regulatory Policy)

Baumol, W.J., Reasonable Rules for Rate Regulation: Plausible Policies
    for an Imperfect World, in the Crisis of Regulatory Commissions,
    W.W. Norton, New York 1970.
Bremen Institute of Shipping Economics, The Future of Liner Shipping,
    Proceedings of an International Symposium, 1974.
Davies, J., The Competitive Environment of Liner Conferences, Maritime
    Policy and Management, Vol.5, No.2. 1978.
Deakin, B.M., Shipping Conferences: Some Economic Aspects of Inter-
    national Regulation, Maritime Studies and Management, Vol.2, No.5.
    1974.

Goss, R.O., <u>The Regulation of International Sea Transport</u>* Royal
Institution of International Affairs. Reprinted in Studies in
Maritime Economics, Cambridge University Press 1968 (*1965).

Goss, R.O., <u>USA Legislation and the Foreign Shipowner: A Critique</u>,*
Journal of Industrial Economics. Reprinted in Studies in Maritime
Economics, Cambridge University Press 1968 (*1963).

HMG Report, <u>Royal Commission on Shipping Rings</u>, Cmnd. 4668, (HMSO)
London 1909.

HMG Report, <u>Report of the Committee of Enquiry into Shipping</u>, The Rt.
Hon. the Viscount Rochdale, Cmnd. 4337, (HMSO) London 1970.

Sletmo, G.K., and Williams, E.W., <u>Liner Conferences in the Container Age</u>,
1981.

US Department of Justice, <u>The Regulated Ocean Shipping Industry</u>, US
Government Printing Office, Washington DC 1977.

US Maritime Administration, <u>The Implementation of the UN Code of
Conduct for Liner Conferences</u>, 1981.

UWIST, <u>Liner Shipping in the US Trades</u>, (A study for CENSA). Reprinted
in Maritime Policy and Management, Vol.5, No.3. 1978.

Wykeman, Magnus, <u>Effects of Cargo Reservation</u>, Marine Policy Vol.4,
No.4. 1980.